HOW TO SPEAK GOODER

Brand-New Rules for Public Speaking in a Digitally Distracted World

Liz Goodgold

Printed and bound in the United States of America
ISBN: 978-0-9776547-2-7
Library of Congress Control Number: 2015903615

BONUS MATERIAL!

Register Your Book Today and Get Valuable Goodies and Bonus Material!

Since I practice what I speech, I don't want to just speak *at* you, but interact *with* you. Please register your book at www.speakgooder.com/bonus and use the code BONU$ to get bonus content and special goodies so that you can continue to speak gooder.

Register now and get:
- Samples of before-and-after bios to more easily write your bio.
- Sample of a fill-in-the-blank order handout that you can emulate.
- Example of my raffle forms so that you can create one too.
- Directions for setting up the room; create an option that works for you!
- Plus, sizzling insider secrets each week to move you forward.

I look forward to staying connected.
Liz Goodgold

To my fab family of Pat, Adam, Mom, Wendy,
and Auntie who make life gooder and funner.

"A good speech is like a woman's skirt:
short enough to hold your attention,
long enough to cover the subject."

—Jonathan Tropper, *This is Where I Leave You*

PREMUMBLE/PREFACE

This Book Is for Entrepreneurs, Employees, and Professional Speakers: Welcome Aboard!

My résumé is a smorgasbord of appetizing jobs throughout the years: brand management at Quaker Oats, lowly book schlepper at Macmillan Publishing Company, gopher and research assistant for Archer Daniels Midland (ADM), brand consultant and CEO of The Nuancing Group, and professional "speecher" and coach at Red Fire Branding for the last 10 years.

Throughout it all, I've had to speak "gooder" to get promoted, get noticed, and get the sale. This book is the secret sauce of my success; it is *not* based upon Toastmasters (I've never even been to a meeting!) or even the "old school" way of speaking, but instead is predicated upon presenting the best YOU to an audience.

I give approximately 75 talks per year, from keynote addresses to breakout sessions to full-day training on branding and speaking. From Meals on Wheels to Warner Brothers to Qualcomm to Pfizer to Abbott Labs, the goal remains consistent: present amazing content that is entertaining, relevant, and interesting enough to get audience members to put down their phone! And, with the advent of Fitbit, Up, and Apple Watch sending nonstop alerts, your talk must mesmerize your audience to either ignore these intrusions or share your content with their followers.

As I transitioned from delivering "rainmaker" speeches (speeches where you don't get paid, but hope to get a prospect in your audience to hire you) to being a paid, professional speaker, I learned the hard way what works … and what doesn't. These lessons have been refined over the years through my FireStarter Speaker Bootcamp. I've coached over 252 entrepreneurs, executives, and employees on "speaking gooder." Whether it's through one-on-one or group coaching, my clients reap the benefits of my knowledge. And now you can too!

YOU Are the Brand and These Are the Brand-New Rules

In all of the training and presentations, my audience is most surprised by the fact that I never teach anyone to imitate me. (*Oy vey*, as my mom would say!) My goal is *not* to teach you to speak like me, but to speak like a better YOU!

It is *your* mannerisms, *your* words, and *your* visual brand that allows your audience to fall in love with you. The Words of Lizdom in this book (yep, it's also the name of my blog) are your guiding principles.

In October 2005, I was contacted by a casting assistant for Simon Cowell; she requested a demo video, as she was casting for a judge for the TV show *American Inventor.* My immediate response was, "OMG! Can't I send you something from the 21st century? Who has a video anymore?" It was an authentic response, and instead of turning her off, it earned me a conversation with the next rung up on the casting ladder. Eventually I spoke with the casting director and urged her to meet with me in person. The very next day I was on the lot at ABC TV shooting a test of the show. At one point, I told an entrepreneur that "his baby was ugly." Simon couldn't stop laughing! And although Mr. Cowell eventually picked someone he'd known for decades, the experience reinforced to me the power of being the brand YOU!

This book is all about kicking to the curb the "old school" of presentation skills. Those rules no longer apply. You can't simply talk "at" people any longer. Today, it's about engagement, entertainment, as much as it is about information. If you only deliver information in a straightforward manner, you will be overlooked in your job, regarded as a second-rate speaker, and dismissed as an entrepreneur.

But if you follow the brand-new rules presented here, you'll be positioned as the expert, employee, or entrepreneur who is committed to embracing the 21st-century rules of communicating.

Separate Chapters for Speakers to Launch Their Speaking Career

Since the goals of speaking are different for paid speakers, employees, and entrepreneurs, I've created independent chapters with relevant material for each target. In the bonus chapters for speakers, you master exactly how to write, sell, and package your speeches. You also get all of the insider know-how on setting up contracts, setting up the room, and setting up the sale. This entire book pays for itself in just one phone call with a meeting planner!

Chapter on How to Earn Praise, Perks, and Promotions as an Employee

In the special chapter for employees, you'll stop turning a presentation in the boardroom to a presentation in the "bored" room! You'll also master how to avoid death by PowerPoint and embrace techniques that work with colleagues and supervisors. Speaking gooder is your secret weapon for avoiding being "made redundant" and is an amazing way to greet new opportunities.

In working with an executive team at Warner Brothers, I initially heard that as employees, they didn't need to sell the speech. After all, attendance at a research meeting, for example, was mandatory.

But, as you'll discover in this book, serving up enticing titles, subject lines, or descriptions for your talks changes the entire perception of your brand. Imagine when colleagues and co-workers can't wait to attend your presentation!

How to Sell You and Your Service as an Entrepreneur Through Speaking

Did you know that the #1 fastest way to get new clients as an entrepreneur is through speaking? Yep, that's the truth! This book arms you with the secrets for selling your services without it ending up as a sales presentation. It allows you to serve up delicious, meaty content while at the same time whetting the audience's appetite for your services.

As you work your way through this book, look for bonus content that is hyperlinked throughout. Also, try the exercises at the end of each chapter. And head on over to www.redfirebranding.com to see expert commentary on what sizzles and fizzles in the world of speaking, branding, and marketing. And follow me on Twitter and YouTube to see weekly updates on what works and what doesn't.

Have a question? Fire away! I'm all ears.

Liz Goodgold
858-550-7000
liz@redfirebranding.com
RedFireBranding.com
Connect with me on Twitter: twitter.com/lizgoodgold
Link with me on LinkedIn: https://www.linkedin.com/in/lizgoodgold
Like me on Facebook: http://www.facebook.com/LizGoodgoldBranding
Enjoy my YouTube Channel http://www.youtube.com/user/LizGoodgold/videos

TABLE OF CONTENTS

PART I

Brand-New Rules of Speaking Today

CHAPTER 1

Branding Rules! Why You Must Deliver the Brand YOU!

The goal of this book is NOT to make you speak like me or even Tony Robbins (although that might be a good thing, and profitable too!). Instead, the goal is for you to speak like a better YOU!

Under no circumstances do I want you to abandon your signature personality and brand. And if you ever meet a coach who wants to drastically change you, run!

I want your authentic self in the spotlight whether you're presenting to eight colleagues or to 800 employees. As Oscar Wilde reportedly said, "Be yourself; everyone else is taken." If you remain true to yourself, you have no fear of being "found out" because you've never projected anything other than the real you. But if you try to be someone you're not, in today's infocentric world, you will be exposed as a fraud.

This book is ideal for executives, entrepreneurs, sales representatives, and employees who must present ideas and talks to others. Speaking is a way to communicate better and more effectively. In fact, good oral communication skills last a long time; it's the gift that keeps on giving, as research shows that good communicators are more likely to get promoted and be rewarded. Have I got your attention yet?

Speaking isn't that hard, and you can do it! Just by flipping through this book, you can see that my approach is an easy one; every element is broken down into bite–sized pieces.

Virtually everyone is an expert in something: therapy, organizing, or investing. Your goal is to impart that knowledge to your audience in a way that sounds like you. But at the same time, make the presentation interesting and entertaining too.

As you climb your career ladder, you'll find that speaking gooder is not a nicety, but a necessity. Solopreneurs are expected to deliver concise and interesting talks; sales reps are expected to deliver a presentation that gets prospects to say yes, and CEOs are expected to rally the troops with a combination of motivation and inspiration.

WORDS OF LIZDOM

Goal of this Book—
My goal is not to teach you to speak like me, but to speak like a better YOU!

Identifying Your Brand DNA

If we're trying to get your talks to sound like you, it's essential that you understand your brand. What's the heart of your brand DNA? Are you witty? Charming? A great number cruncher? These elements of you must be preserved and presented to your audience.

The exercises at the end of this chapter under *Get Gooder … Get Going!* guide you toward discovering your brand DNA. After all, branding is not what you are; it's how others perceive you. You can then layer these personality traits into all of your presentations.

Exaggerate Your Brand DNA

I remember a number of years ago coaching the great storyteller Kelly Swanson. She was concerned that if she moved to a main-stage speaker, she would have to give up her Southern accent or her favorite pair of boots. I exclaimed, "No! They are part of what makes up the brand YOU! Your goal as a speaker is not just to *protect* your signature style, but to *project* it."

The exact same concept holds true for speaker Laura Meyerovich; she embraces her Russian accent vs. running from it.

Brand by Color

Our world revolves around color. Next time your friends get ready to prepare their cup of coffee, watch how they look for their sweetener: "blue" (Equal), "pink" (Sweet'N Low), "green" (Stevia), or yellow (Splenda). They might even go so far as to ask a waiter if they have any of the "blue stuff."

In January 2015, college football changed its championship format so that it set the stage for Ohio State University vs. the University of Oregon. The Oregon Ducks had been on a wild ride, often with more media and crowd attention on its vibrant green and yellow uniforms than on its fast-paced offense! But when the team took to the field against the flaming backdrop of red-shirted Buckeye fans, it was wearing white! White is the antithesis of the brand it created. The excitement was gone, fans looked ridiculous in bright green jerseys, and the team lost 42–20.

This phenomenon of branding by color takes place even in the field of medicine. Patients will often tell their doctors that they take a little blue pill or a big yellow pill. Pharmaceutical manufacturers have the opportunity to use color to help consumers, doctors, and to reinforce their image.

Nexium has branded itself as the "purple pill" and even uses that phrase as its domain! Nuprin was the first drug to introduce a rust-colored pill. Now that color is ubiquitous as the standard color of ibuprofen, as evidenced by all similarly-hued generic competitors.

And Levoxyl, a thyroid medicine, according to Dr. Wendy Schilling, uses a stroke of branding genius by color coding its pills according to dosage.

Apparently other women besides me are looking for that robin's egg blue–colored box during the holidays, signifying a gift from T&Co.—Tiffany. Just seeing the color triggers a 20 percent increase in the heart rate of American women. How's that for emotionally connecting with the brand?

WORDS OF LIZDOM

Definition of Branding—
Branding is not what you say you are; it is how others *perceive* you.

And the color of the car we drive matters. A whopping 39 percent of car buyers will walk out of a showroom if their desired car color is not in stock! Currently, every GM car comes in 22 colors, and almost 75 percent of its cars come in orange. Clearly, orange is trending this year.

New Zealand uses the color black fairly consistently to identify its sports teams: All Blacks is the name of the national rugby team, the women's national rugby team is the Black Ferns, the men's basketball team is the Tall Blacks, and the field hockey team is the Black Sticks.

The singer Pink certainly created her brand name based upon her signature hair color. But it was her hard-hitting style, no-holds-barred lyrics, and outspoken interviews that enabled her to build her brand image beyond her hairstyle. Today she boasts a platinum blonde look.

Since color acts as part of our personality, it's no surprise that as we develop, change, or even age, our color preferences change as well. For example, in 1993 Susan Macaulay moved from her home country of

Canada to accompany her husband to Dubai. For 10 years, she looked for work and lived a very comfortable existence. Then, on the spur of the moment, she accepted a challenge by the not-for-profit Gulf for Good to tackle a six-day, 120-kilometer trek on the wild side of the Great Wall of China. To get in shape for the trek, she had to create a healthier version of herself. After losing 20 pounds and conquering both the Great Wall of China and Mount Kinabalu, she completely switched her wardrobe to body-hugging clothes and adopted the color pink as her signature color—a color she used to despise!

I remember meeting the founder of a "women in business" yellow pages directory-type company in Chicago. Her image is burned into my mind: a spectacular yellow suit with a black silk blouse. She literally was her own walking mascot!

Author and speaker Jeffrey Gitomer has built an empire out of color coding his books: *Little Gold Book of YES! Attitude, Little Red Book of Selling, Little Black Book of Connections,* etc.

See about adopting a signature color. A recent study published in the *Wall Street Journal* demonstrated that if job candidates wore the same color suit on both the first and second interviews, they were 20 percent more likely to get hired than candidates who arbitrarily changed colors. The lesson? A signature color helps us remember a name.

Brand by a Signature Look

Actress Lisa Rinna finally admitted to blowing up her lips to their extreme look today. But, as she says, those lips gave her a career! Take away her kisser and you're left with just another pretty brunette in Hollywood.

Zooey Deschanel credits her success to finally embracing bangs and bold eyeliner. She was forgettable as a blonde. Hint: Try to recognize her in the movie *Elf.*

J. Lo and Beyoncé have embraced their "bootylicious" bodies and find a way to constantly show them off. Shania Twain turned heads and boosted her status and sales when she belted out "Man, I Feel Like a Woman" at the Grammy Awards with gloves, short skirt, and thigh-high boots. This look was recently updated for her sold-out Vegas shows too.

Speaker Larry Winget would never grow his hair, discard his cowboy boots, remove his earrings, or forget his cowboy shirts. Ariana Grande's high ponytail is her trademarked look. Just as Larry King donned suspenders, Mister Rogers wore a cardigan sweater, and Crystal Gayle never cut her hair, you and I need to adopt a signature look. Get it, perfect it, and don't change it!

Liz Goodgold: A Case Study in Branding

Let me share how I project my brand DNA throughout my wardrobe, website, vocabulary, and speaking events. Some of these items are covered later in this book, but let me summarize them here. Again, these are the items that work for me. You must decide what works for you.

Visual Brand

As you may have guessed, my company name, Red Fire Branding, was inspired by my hair color. It's also commonly represented in fireworks, which seems appropriate, as I believe hot brands spark new ideas. I virtually always wear a red jacket when I speak. And, yes, my closet boasts at least 16 different styles. Of course, the jacket matches my nail polish and even my Jawbone UP fitness tracker. Ditto for my tote bag and at least a dozen pairs of comfortable red shoes from Nine West to Cole Haan.

External Branding

Yes, I drive a flame-red car, and a Mercedes has been my brand of choice for the last ten years. If you see me behind the wheel with the license plate RedFire, please give me a friendly honk!

Brand Vocabulary

I play upon both my first and last names. You'll see my blog entitled Words of Lizdom, special packages called the Bronze, Silver, and Goodgold offerings, events occurring before my time as in the "pre-Elizabethan era," and even the title of this book stems from half of my last name, Gooder. Cathie Black, former publisher of *USA Today*, named her book *Basic Black*, based upon her name. See if you can find inspiration from your name as well.

Brand Metaphors

Similarly, my bio claims that I am a fiery redhead. I offer coaching packages called Red Hot/Ad Hoc Coaching and FireStarter, and sizzling specials.

Brand Music

I often walk onto the stage to "Burning Down the House," "This Girl Is On Fire," or "Feeling Hot, Hot, Hot" by the Merrymen.

Audience Treats

My peeps are rewarded for participating with Red Hots, Hot Tamales, Fireballs, Atom Balls, Vosges Red Fire chocolate bars, and any other hot red item I can find.

Attitude

With my big-as-life personality, it's hard for me to show up at a networking event as a wallflower or, gosh forbid, depressed. My gung-ho attitude is simply a part of me.

Get Gooder ... Get Going!

1. **Discover Your Brand DNA**—Send an email to clients, customers, colleagues, or vendors asking them for seven to ten adjectives (descriptive words) about you. Now do the exact same exercise for yourself. If you are a consistent brand, you should see clear overlap; you are seeing yourself the way others see you. If not, you must tackle this branding gap and create alignment between how you want to be seen and how others see you.

2. **Take Stock of Your Wardrobe**—Look at your closet and check out any color trends. Since you are the brand, you should pick colors that are already near and dear to your heart.

3. **Determine if You Can Create a Signature Sound or Song**—Is there music that works for you? Can you warm up your audience with it?

CHAPTER 2

Your Visual Brand: Dressing to Brand Out, Stand Out, and Cash In as a Speaker

"Dress for success" was the mantra in the late '70s, but it applies to all speakers, because there are functional and psychological effects of what you wear as a speaker. Think of your wardrobe as part of your visual brand.

Ladies: Functional Considerations of What You Wear

Let me put it this way: your work wardrobe must work for you! And women have special considerations that I'm addressing here.

Before you settle on your outfit for your talk, make sure you can raise your arms, stretch your body, and be 100 percent comfortable in the outfit. Nix anything too short or too tight. And shoes can make or break your event. If your feet hurt, it's impossible to give a flawless presentation. Check that you can stand comfortably in your shoes and move effortlessly. I love my Jimmy Choos just as much as the next girl, but I usually opt for cushy and functional shoes from Cole Haan that have the patented Nike Air inserts. And if you're looking for a line of shoes that are both comfortable and fashionable, check out Taryn Rose, Vionic, and Paul Green.

I'll never forget when Lisa Schulteis, Infusionsoft expert, and my web designer, (www.electralime.com), told me about a speaker who bombed. The reason? It appeared as if her feet were killing her the entire time. The pain in her feet seemed to literally zap the energy from her talk.

9

If you're speaking to a large group, you're likely to be set up with a head-worn, wireless microphone. This microphone is a headset that goes around the back of your head or ear and then extends with a slim microphone near your jawline (think of the infamous Madonna outfit with the ponytail, cones, and microphone, and you'll get the picture). Earrings—especially dangly ones—will click against the microphone, driving you and your audience crazy. Beware: ask your organizer in advance what type of microphone you'll be using, and skip the earrings if using a head-worn mic.

Noise in general will distract your audience, so necklaces, earrings, or sleeves that jingle or jangle are verboten. In fact, anything that takes away from you as the star is best left at home. Instead, focus on a color or outfit that simply reinforces the brand you!

Head-worn wireless microphones and wireless lavalier microphones both have a battery pack that needs to be attached to you in some way. Typically, they're easily attached to the waistband of pants or skirts. Warning: if you're wearing a dress without a belt, the battery pack will need to be connected to the back of your dress or inside your dress or on the back of your bra. All of these types of attachments can distort the front of your dress and are terribly uncomfortable. I gave up on wearing dresses while speaking that don't have a thick belt just because of this bizarre issue. Laura Van Tyne of Crystal Pointe Media, who speaks on self-publishing, laughingly remembers how a silk dress coupled with a microphone became her nemesis, as it too easily made her overexposed.

WORDS OF LIZDOM

Don't Let Fashion Overwhelm Function—
Ensure that your clothing
and shoes work for you. Check to make
sure nothing is too short, too tight,
or too uncomfortable.

No Bad Hair Days Allowed

In our always "on" society, there's no way to escape photos being taken of you with or without your permission. If you're speaking, then your audience is taking photos—guaranteed. So you must dress and style yourself so that you're happy with the photos that appear on Instagram, Facebook, Twitter, and Pinterest.

Confirm the Dress Code

Before committing to your speaking outfit, it's a good idea to confirm the dress code and then plan accordingly. When I was giving a keynote for Unipharm in Kona, Hawaii, I made sure that everybody would be in tropical-casual dress. I didn't want to show up in a very proper red suit if the conference attendees were all in shorts and flip-flops. I'd not only feel foolish, but also immediately create a disconnect between me and my audience.

You might also adopt the rule of dressing just a little bit better than the audience members. You don't want to dress so far "upscale" from your audience that you are perceived as unapproachable. Remember that you want to interact and engage with them both at this event and in the future. If your outfit reeks of overt wealth, for example, your potential clients or employers might just tune out!

Adopt a Signature Style

Sometimes you can literally wear your brand. If you are speaking as a scientist, you might want to look like one. In fact, Clinique was one of the first cosmetic companies to require a white lab coat. It does a great job of connecting the scientific, clinical approach to makeup with their brand name. Steve Jobs adopted the uniform of a mock turtleneck coupled with Levi's and his trademark glasses. After his passing in 2013, many devotees dressed up as the founder of Apple for Halloween.

Your signature speaking uniform could be a chef's toque (restaurant) or even a tuxedo (wedding disc jockey). See what makes sense for you and your brand.

WORDS OF LIZDOM

Imitation Is Great Flattery—
You are not a brand if you can't be imitated. How would someone dress if they decided to be you for Halloween?

Consistency Is Key

The most important element throughout your visual brand is consistency. How you look today is how you must look tomorrow.

I remember going to a speaking event in Tucson, and the temperature was 118 degrees. Of course, for the airplane ride I dressed lightly and pulled my bundle of red hair on top of my head. When the driver arrived to pick me up at the airport, he claimed not to recognize me. The minute my hair tumbled down, my universal image was restored. I am not kidding here: you must look like your photo—always.

You don't have to adopt a signature color like I do with the color red, but you do want a look that is consistent. Milo Shapiro appears in white suspenders, and many female speakers just always look pulled together. As a woman, I find a black base with a burst of color on top is effortless. Note: Wearing all black usually causes you to fade into the stage and curtains in a big venue, so opt for something besides the entire Johnny Cash look.

Will a Hat Work?

Hats also remain a mark of distinction. Alan Jackson wears a white cowboy hat when it seems that every other country singer has opted for the ubiquitous black hat. Those of us who revere wine instantly recognize Mike Grgich with his trademark black beret. Congressional representative Frederica Wilson fought the rules in her home state of Florida so that she could continue to don her signature hats.

Get Gooder ... Get Going!

1. **Create a Signature Style**—It doesn't have to be a hat, scarf, or even color, but you should look pretty similar at all of your speaking events.

2. **Determine if You Have a Signature Color**—Review your closet and check out any color trends. Since you are the brand, you should pick colors that are already near and dear to your heart.

3. **Ask About the Dress Code**—Make sure to question your meeting planner about the formality of the event. If it's in summer or a tropical locale, expect the answer to be "biz casual."

CHAPTER 3

How to Get to the Holy Grail of Branding:
Flawless Recall

Every time you give a speech, your goal is flawless recall. If you give a rip-roaring speech but no one remembers your name, you have failed! If your goal is to get promoted but you remain forgettable, you aren't building a dream career. If you're trying to triple your entrepreneurial business but your name can't be googled, you've come up short.

To ensure that your name doesn't fade into oblivion, here are nine techniques to ensure flawless recall.

1. Have Someone Introduce You

No matter how small your group, it pays great dividends to have someone else introduce you. It allows for your credibility to be established without boasting. After all, imagine how it would sound if you kept saying, "And then I accomplished this, and then I achieved that ..." At the same time, an introduction affords your audience the opportunity to hear your name a few times and even learn how to pronounce it correctly.

2. Teach Them How to Pronounce Your Name

I've found out the hard way that a good many Americans are dyslexic. How? I've been introduced as Liz Goldgood. (BTW, it's GOODGold.) So my introduction now says: "Here's a speaker who is as good as gold, Liz Goodgold." It reminds the introducer to utter my name correctly.

Pronouncing your name correctly is not insignificant. Why? Because if folks are afraid to pronounce your name correctly, they won't; no one wants to look foolish by saying a name the wrong way. And if you want to build your brand by word-of-mouth buzz, it's impossible if folks are afraid to say your name! In your mind, think of the Destiny's Child song "Say My Name."

For all these reasons, I make all my clients create a device to ensure their name is pronounced correctly. Quick, how would you say Gail Iwaniak? How 'bout if I told you it rhymes with "Gail, I want a Pontiac!" Would that help you remember the founder of Stuffology?

Esther Weinberg of MindLight Group shows her name as WINE-Berg so that announcers don't say WIN-Berg. Dr. Alok Kalia, author of *Don't Take Dieting Advice From a Skinny Person*, offers up this tip: "Alok, rhymes with a joke." Get it?

3. Look Like Your Photo

The speaking world isn't a variation of a dating site whereby your photo is 20 years and 20 pounds ago. Instead, how you look today must be how your photo looks today. If your company is still promoting an antiquated photo of you, it's time to petition for a new headshot. And if you're the entrepreneur, ensure that you take new photos at least every five years.

You'll also note that the visual brand has become more important, as we discussed in chapter 2. Headshots are no longer simply a smiling face; full length and action photos are critical too. The goal is to show a hint of your personality. You can see the entire scope of my recent photos over here: http://www.redfirebranding.com/speaking/see-liz-in-action/photo-gallery/

As my client and brilliant photographer Stefanie Blue of True Blue Portrait states: "Today, a photo is more than just a basic headshot for your bio page. It's about being the expert, the leader, the cool chick—the local celebrity. People want to be able to say, 'I know her!' And they do that when you appear so polished and professional that you take on a commercial edge with your image branding and become a celebrated personality."

4. Create a Handout

A handout isn't just to leave a lasting impression; its goal is also to reinforce your brand name with the audience. Of course, then, include your first and last name and all your contact info. (For rules about handouts, please see chapter 8.)

WORDS OF LIZDOM

Holy Grail of Branding—
People must remember you in order to do business with you. People must remember you in order to *refer* business to you.

5. Wear a Name Tag

Attendees often overlook the power of a name tag. It reinforces your brand name and teaches others how to spell it. I recommend to all my clients that they buy a custom-created, magnetic one. In fact, this past holiday season, I gave every client one! Wouldn't you rather wear an elegant, logo-embedded name tag than a peel-and-stick version that ruins your clothes? **Homework**: Get a name badge today!

AND, this is your reminder to always wear your name tag on your right lapel so that your shoulder (and name tag) turns toward the person when you're shaking hands. In other words, you are making visual contact, physical contact, and allowing a stranger to read your name badge all at the same time.

I wear my name badge before, during, and after the event where I am speaking, but not when on stage speaking. It detracts from the visual appearance and often interferes with microphone placement; just remember to put it back on for the remainder of the event.

6. Use Your Own Name in the Third Person

My talks are constantly peppered with stories about my mom, son, and husband. Intentionally, I'll relay a story where an exasperated family member turns to me and exclaims, "Liz, but what were you thinking?" It serves the story by making clear who is speaking while at the same time reinforcing my first name.

7. Have a Visual Reminder of Your Name

If you're an author, you have an easy way to trigger name recall: simply hold up your book! I remember hearing the story of renowned speaker Ken Blanchard flying off from our hometown of San Diego to give a talk prior to 9/11. He apparently forgot his identification, so he ran to the airport bookstore and bought his own book. As he whisked through security, he used his photo on the back of his book to prove his identity!

If you're the keynote speaker, there is typically "room signage" associated with the event. This term refers to signs on the podium, signs throughout the room, or even a simple sign next to the coffee-pot with words such as "Thanks to ZXYZ Company for sponsoring our coffee break."

You too can maximize your brand exposure by draping a table with your customized, branded tablecloth, using inexpensive picture frames with special offers, or even investing in a stand-up display with your picture on it. All of these items help burn your brand into prospects' minds.

8. Invent Brand Phrases That Reinforce Your Name

At my talks, you'll often hear me not only share my words of Lizdom, but joke about the Goodgolden rules of raffles. I even offer three coaching packages: bronze, silver, and Goodgold! My client and the founder of Stress Be Gong, Teri Wilder, often sings a line or two in her talks and calls this "Teri-oake!" Gail Kraft turns her name into a verb with the brand Kraft Bravery.

Radio personalities Jeff and Jer have the "Jerantee." They guarantee that you'll like the movie they recommend or they'll send you your money back! *So You Think You Can Dance* judge Mary Murphy exclaims, "Lord, have Murphy!" Even tennis champion Roger Federer has gotten into the game, wearing T-shirts in preparation for his 2015 Australian Open with the word "Betterer." Love it!

Raving fans have created these names:

Brand	Branded Fan Name
Glee	Gleeks
Lady Gaga	Little Monsters
Peet's Coffee	Peetniks
Justin Bieber	Beliebers
Hannibal	Fannibals
Clay Aiken	Claymates
Joan Rivers	Joan Rangers
Benedict Cumberbatch	Cumberb**ch
Shania Twain	Twainiacs
Beyoncé	BeyHive

WORDS OF LIZDOM

Teach Them How to Pronounce Your Name Correctly—
If people can't pronounce your name correctly, they won't!

9. Use Signature Phrases and Epigrams

Just as I believe the world should be funner and you should speak gooder, the mnemonic technique here is to get people to repeat your memorable phrases. Business Coach Mary "Money" Rogers reminds her attendees that "It's all about the leads." Home Exchange Expert Shelley Miller intones: "Come for the savings, stay for the lifestyle." Speaker Sheryl Roush gives presentations with "sparkletude." Rachel Ray taught us that EVOO means Extra Virgin Olive Oil, and Emeril Lagasse never tires of exclaiming, "Bam!"

A perfect example of someone with a unique and indelible brand is Garrison Keillor, long-running host of *A Prairie Home Companion*. Every week he delivers a monologue focused on the fictional town of Lake Wobegon that always ends with the signature phrase, "All the women are strong, all the men are good-looking, and all the children are above average."

I was honored over the holidays to receive the most beautiful gift from talented copywriter Anne McColl. (In fact, she calls herself the best damn copywriter, and I agree!) She put together an entire package of my epigrams. The list includes:

- Speak like your peeps.
- Brand out to stand out!
- Go from Ho-Hum to Gung-Ho.

See the beautiful imagery and all of the rotating phrases on my website.

Get Gooder ... Get Going!

1. **Create a Device to Teach People How to Pronounce Your Name**—Whether it's a rhyme, an expression, or a mnemonic device, find a way to get your name on everyone's lips ... the right way!

2. **Keep a List of Your Epigrams**—As you build your list of signature phrases, you build your brand. You also keep others from stealing them.

3. **Get a Name Badge**—Today! It's time to throw away the peel-and-stick name tags that ruin your clothes and appear as the polished professional that you are. We use www.namify.com, but there are tons of easy and affordable options online.

PART II
Preparing the Speech

CHAPTER 4

Speaking in a Digitally Distracted, Twitter-Happy, Textus Interruptus World

Everything you learned about speaking is wrong! If you're accustomed to the old adage of "Tell them what you're going to tell them and then tell them what you told them," now is the time to kick that epigram to the curb!

Five Reasons Why Speaking Must Change:

1. The Age of Boring Is Over

Everyone today feels overwhelmed and overworked. The last item on most of our agendas is to sit through a boring newscast or educational seminar. Even network channels have morphed their news broadcasts into a hybrid format blending information, education, and entertainment, creating "edutainment."

2. The Entertainment Bar Is High

Even amateur videos today look sleek and polished. Further, the success of TED Talks and TED Talk Radio have proven that speakers can be entertaining. Viewers today make a quick decision as to whether they'll tune in ... or out!

3. Technology Is Always Within Reach

Our phones and iPads are never far from reach, let alone out of our hands. As a result, speakers today must be interesting enough to grab attention and hold it. They must also foster such interaction that your audience is tweeting away, further boosting your brand and buzz. As social media expert Danica Kombol says: "We live in a mobile/digital age. The sound of applause to me is tap tap tap."

4. Technology Is Always On

Thanks to the introduction of the Apple Watch, texts, tweets, and talk is always easily accessible. Audience members don't even have to take out their phone anymore!

5. Attention Deficit Disorder Is Rampant

Whether it's a medical condition or the temporary malaise of your audience, multitasking afflicts everyone today; they are taking on too many tasks at once and not paying strong attention to any of them! Speakers must make fewer, yet stronger, points. And with more wearable technology, from the Fitbit to the Up to the Apple Watch, individuals are buzzed with alerts about their health, new messages, or a reminder to get up and move.

Embrace the New Economy of Social Media NOW!

If you keep waiting for Twitter to go away, you're going to be out of time and luck. Facebook, now with over a billion users, and Pinterest, with over 70 million active users, prove that social media is here to stay. The conversation continues either with or without you. Join the discussion and you can monitor, engage, contribute, and direct it. If you remain out of the loop, it's as if people are talking behind your back. Even the Securities and Exchange Commission (SEC) now recognizes Twitter as a legitimate stream of communication for reporting performance!

Yes, you may be overworked and overwhelmed and don't want any more things to do on your plate. However, ignoring social media platforms pigeonholes you as an "old adult who just doesn't get it." And it's hard to get hired today in any capacity without social media acumen.

As CEO of the North San Diego Business Chamber Debra Rosen said so succinctly: "Even if I'm not hiring you as the social media director, you must know how to engage, post, and connect with today's audiences in order to remain employable." Don't forget: Millennials (those born between 1983 and 2001) represent almost 25 percent of Americans. These are the folks who grew up with their fingers seemingly surgically attached to technology. Communicating effectively with them requires that you speak *their* language and master *their* tools. And your boss or next client just might be an iPhone genius like whiz kid Nick D'Aloisio, who sold his app to Yahoo for $30 million.

Start Tweeting the News!

Instead of asking participants to put away their cell phones, encourage them to share the new currency of the web: hot information. Display your Twitter handle on your PowerPoint or whiteboard and create a hashtag for your speeches. Make sure to post the Wi-Fi access to encourage rampant interaction.

Another way of adapting to the new social media economy is to verbally highlight key information when it's relayed. It's as if you're providing Cliff's Notes as you speak. You are framing key points so that they are remembered and easily adapted for Facebook and other social media. You might hear me say, "Here's something to tweet: Speak Like Your Peeps." You're not insulting your audience, but helping them find your major points.

Following is a sample stream from the Women Business Owners Conference. The hashtag keeps all of the information from the same event together while at the same time building your personal brand and reputation.

- People have to remember us to do business with us @lizgoodgold #WBOC13
- Be the brand that never goes on sale RT @SantiGianna #WBOC13
- @lizgoodgold The 30 second speech is over; time for the 7-second hook.

We live in a visual society, and photos are also critical. Facebook research shows that streams with photos get 40 percent more readership. Pose for photos before your talk, pose during your talk, and mingle afterwards. These photos extend your reach and reputation on Instagram, Pinterest, and other social media outlets.

WORDS OF LIZDOM

The Old Rules of Speaking Don't Work—
The new Internet economy demands new rules
and new tools. Every speech must have
a tweetable sound bite.

Seven Ways to Boost Interactivity

No longer can we speak *at* an audience; we must speak *with* an audience. Just as the Internet is all about dialogue, the same is true of our audiences: they must be able to chime in, discuss, and digest new information. The new speakers of today must create an unforgettable experience. Felena Hanson, founder of Hera Hub, always creates an interactive exercise, even at her TEDx talk. In that talk, she had her audience write down their one action step that they were committed to doing. She then mailed them back their commitment to themselves exactly one year later. Cool, right?

To prove the point that phonics doesn't work with learning disabled students, Dr. Suki Stone, author of *Rethinking Reading Strategies*, asks her audience to spell onomatopoeia. Needless to say, virtually no one gets it right. But, when the audience uses their smartphones to get the correct spelling, it clearly demonstrates the power of technology.

Presenters can encourage maximum participation with these techniques:

1. Introduce Yourself to Everyone as They Arrive

Most attendees are a little tentative when they arrive; they're unsure what to expect or who else will be there. I try to reassure the attendees by introducing myself, shaking hands, asking questions, and making them feel welcome from the get-go. My interaction with them at the beginning boosts their participation and interaction at my session.

2. Facilitate Questions and Answers

Asking questions of your audience is underrated. Why? Most presenters either ask rhetorical questions (a big no-no; see chapter 6 for more information) or forget to allow the particpants to answer and then address those specific questions! It also bears repeating that you should ensure that your group feels safe asking questions; remind the group about the ground rules too, such as, "There are no stupid questions."

3. Solve Problems as a Group

Instead of merely asking for a show of hands or asking a simple question, tackle a common problem together. Use a whiteboard so that the audience can see the progress. For example, during a presentation to World Trade Centers, I asked the group how it could demonstrate its brand values to visitors. Each answer sparked more ideas as we addressed the problem together.

4. Create a Role-Play

Role-playing is one of the best ways to allow the audience to "practice what I speech!" In my workshops on creating a successful paid speaking career, I have participants make mock phone calls to meeting planners. Universally, role-playing is one of the best tools around.

5. Bring an Audience Member to the Front

Having a participant "play" with you and your information is a great way to loosen up the event and add a laugh. I always *ask* for a volunteer; under no circumstances should you take an unwilling participant. As we know, there are shy wallflowers who hate to be embarrassed, so let the class clowns and big personalities share the stage.

You can coach the volunteer in the moment, ask questions, solve a problem, or even have them act out a role. I remember having three volunteers come to the stage to act out the panel judges from *American Idol* to show the power of your personal brand. My actors killed it with impersonations of Randy Jackson, Nicki Minaj, and Mariah Carey.

6. Allow One Audience Member to Help Another

Even if you are leading the presentation, it doesn't mean that you have to have all of the answers. It takes a little finesse, but it's worth practicing the art of asking the group for a question and then allowing another audience member to answer it. Don't forget to applaud the attempted answer, whether or not you agree with it. The minute you criticize, you shut down the hope of future engagement.

7. Create an Exercise

In any type of small-scale seminar (fewer than 75 attendees), create a way to have participants put the theory presented into action. For example, I believe that every person in business needs a compelling seven-second hook. This hook is a quick way to introduce yourself rather than the old-school idea of a 30-second infomercial. After all, who has that kind of time? Client Jenn Harris, founder of High Heel Golfer, has the hook: "I teach female executives to make more green on the greens." Book coach Bethany Kelly simply says: "I turn experts into authors."

To further good takeaways from a talk, I create an interactive exercise whereby members pair up in groups of two to help each other devise their hook. It reinforces key concepts. As I explain later in this book, make sure to set up your room to optimize interaction.

In order to achieve a successful interactive exercise, remember these rules:

1. Explain the Exercise Completely

Confused participants spread confusion like wildfire. Ensure that your directions are abundantly clear.

2. Mix It Up

Include a variety of partners; make sure to have a few activities that are solo acts, as well as groups from two to eight.

3. Remain in Control

Have a method for taking back control so that the room doesn't run amok. I often bring a gong to ring, which is not only fun, but also creates a nice "headwhip" effect, as in "What's that?" In other words, people aren't expecting the sound of a gong, so they whip their head around to find out where the sound is coming from.

4. Devise a Method for Creating Teams

Don't forget to inject fun into selecting teams. Here's an idea: bring an oversize deck of cards and have everyone choose a card upon entering the room. Eventually, form a team with all of the kings, jacks, tens, etc. … Or, if you want larger teams, have them divide by suits (spades, diamonds, hearts, and clubs).

5. Decide Who Goes First

Again, in order to conduct the exercise calmly, pre-determine how to decide who starts first. You can do everything from using birthdays, to hair length, to height. It doesn't matter, as long as folks know exactly what to do.

6. Provide a Timeframe

Example: "Go ahead and brainstorm as many names as you can for the next two minutes until I say stop."

7. Debrief the Exercise

Often, the great value of an exercise is learning from others. As a result, make sure to have groups share with the group as a whole. And remember, not everyone or every group has to share, but enough of them need to in order to provide good learning for the group.

8. Reward Amazing Efforts

Provide little gifts and treats for the team with the most answers, the most innovative solution, the wildest idea, etc.

WORDS OF LIZDOM

Add a Fun Factor to Every Talk—
Every talk can benefit from a little more fun. Think about props, games, food, or anything that adds a little levity.

Adding the Fun Factor

Your goal as a presenter is to add fun throughout. Think about the routine elements in a talk and then spice it up! For example, virtually all small seminars allow the participants to introduce themselves. I do too, BUT not at the beginning; it sucks all the energy out of the room. Instead, I do it after delivering at least 45 minutes of solid content and then adding a fun factor. Sometimes I have folks contribute their funniest interaction with a celebrity, their favorite color or number, their craziest first job, etc. I'll never forget the employee from Eagle Legacy Credit Union who fessed up to being Raymond Burr's private driver or the colleague who had Tom Petty play at her wedding. Allow your audience to share, become vulnerable, and let the energy soar!

Another fun-factor contributor is candy. Yes, I'm aware of the evils of sugar, but in my 15 years as a speaker, nothing works quite as well as chocolate. Here are a few examples: I did a talk on Valentine's Day and gave participants sweet treats of chocolate hearts. Or, if someone delivers a sizzling performance, I reward them with my signature Hot Tamales, Red Fire Bars by Voges, Fireballs, or even Big Red gum.

It not only gives me a treat to throw, but it also reinforces my brand.

WORDS OF LIZDOM

**Never Have Participants
Introduce Themselves at the Beginning—**
In seminars with fewer than 25 participants,
it makes sense to give participants a short time to
introduce themselves, BUT never at the start
of your talk. It immediately sucks the
energy out of the room.

Other speakers who I've had the joy of working with have used these devices:

Henry DeVries

Oh Henry bars (naturally!)

Sky Jeannette

As a proponent of Juice Plus+, she throws oranges or apples to her audience, which is utterly consistent with her brand.

Show, Don't Tell

Another way to have fun is to use props on stage. Barry Cohen, of AdLab, has a flair for the dramatic. He asks his audience if they'd like to see some "big money" right away, and then hands out oversized fake bills. He then counters by asking who wanted to see some "smaller bills," and then hands out miniature fake money. It's a great way to engage and laugh.

Get Gooder ... Get Going!

1. **Join the Social Media Revolution**—Every entrepreneur, employee, or executive must be on LinkedIn. Ensure that your bio is accurate and current. If you need help, I offer bio creation on my website.

2. **Pick One Other Social Media Network**—In addition to LinkedIn, join one other social media network and get good at it. It's better to be an active Twitter user, for example, who posts ten times per day and has 10,000 followers than an occasional Instagram user with few followers.

3. **Incorporate Social Media into Your Talks**—Develop a hashtag for the event so that participants can follow the conversation.

4. **Find Fun Foods**—Be on the lookout now for what will become your signature item.

5. **Try Out Your Exercises**—If you're trying a new interactive activity, conduct a guinea-pig trial; in can be before someone else's event, just as long as it works!

CHAPTER 5

How to Tell a Story and How to *Sell* a Story

We all forget data, but we never forget stories. Think for a minute about "The Boy Who Cried Wolf" or "The Tortoise and the Hare." Quick, do you remember the lesson? You betcha! Data strays, but stories stay.

Speaker Sarita Maybin, the author of *If You Can't Say Something Nice, What Do You Say?* has been telling the following signature story about her daughter and green Jell-O for 15 years!

I was standing in the kitchen fixing my special Sunday breakfast. This is always a big deal, because I don't cook a big breakfast every day. My daughter, who was four years old at the time, came into the kitchen, opened the refrigerator, and noticed a four-pack of green Jell-O.

"Mommy," she asked, "May I have a green Jell-O?"

At this point I hesitated, contemplating whether or not I wanted her to have it. After all, I was fixing breakfast. However, I said, "OK, you may have one." She took the Jell-O, slurped it up and returned only moments later. "May I have another one?"

This time I said "No!" She dropped to the floor in a tantrum. She shrieked in a high-pitched, shrill, whiny voice that sounded much like the sound of fingernails scratching against a chalkboard, "I want Jell-O, I want Jell-O!"

As my daughter writhed on the floor in a full-blown tantrum, I looked at her. Without sympathy, I said, "Crying will not help you!"

Let's talk now about the husband.

Husband (shouting from the living room): "Give her the @# Jell-O!"*

Sarita: "Honey, I'd rather not give it to her. I'm fixing breakfast."

Husband: "What's the BIG DEAL! Just give her the Jell-O!"

Sarita: "I'd rather not."

Do you sense a conflict brewing?

At that point, husband and I are at each other's throats.

"Jell-O!"

"No Jell-O!"

"Jell-O!"

"No Jell-O!"

"What's wrong with this picture?" I asked myself. "I make a living teaching others conflict resolution, teamwork, dealing with negativity, and communication skills. Surely I was NOT engaged in a conflict over … GREEN JELL-O!!!?"

Then it occurred to me. The most important aspect of conflict resolution is to

figure out the real agenda.

So … what might have been husband's not-so-hidden agenda in this Sunday morning scenario?

You guessed it … SHUT THE CHILD UP!

And what might have been my agenda?

"I'm cooking breakfast over this hot stove … somebody better eat!" (Ego)

"Crying will NOT be rewarded!" (Discipline)

"I'm the mommy here!" (Control)

"I want those other Jell-Os for myself!" (Self-Serving)

"Shut husband up!" (Power/Turf)

This is no different than how conflict happens outside of the kitchen and inside the workplace.

Notice how this story is taken from everyday life; it has enough detail that we can imagine the tantrum the daughter is throwing while not overwhelming us with extraneous detail, such as what Sarita was making for breakfast. But most importantly, the brilliance of the story is in how it seamlessly backs up the point that conflict can happen anywhere.

It doesn't matter that Sarita's daughter is now out of college; the story and the lesson remain timeless. And therein lies the crux of the issue: Any type of story works as long as you demonstrate a key lesson. Stories without a lesson are just a waste of time.

WORDS OF LIZDOM

Data strays, but stories stay.

Here's an unforgettable story from humorist speaker Colette Carlson:

Do any of you know someone who deals with their stress by taking it out on others? I do.

I can still remember the moment like it was yesterday—even though it was over a decade ago. I was going to night school to get my Masters in Human Behavior and it had been one of THOSE days. All you want to do at the end of the day is plunk your bottom on the couch, zone out, and pour yourself a nice, cool, refreshing beverage (said under breath: glass of wine). Ironically, the class I was taking that night was on the Effects of Drugs and Alcohol!

I'm trying to get to my night class on time and trying to jam and cram too much in too little time. So I'm throwing a load of laundry in, trying to slap something edible on the table, and my youngest is clinging to my leg crying, "I don't want you to go." I grab a cup of coffee on my way out the door so I can even stay awake for the class, jump in my car and start to back out of the driveway. When I look up, I see my two little girls running and screaming after me like the paparazzi on a Kardashian ... and perhaps, like you, in a similar situation ... I just wanted to hit the gas! But, I didn't. Instead I slam on the brakes, buzz down my window, and stare down my two defenseless daughters at the same time I channel Joan Crawford—Mommie Dearest herself, "What do you two want now?" And I'll never forget it. My oldest's eyes fill with tears and her lower lip does that trembling thing and she says, "Mommy, we just came to tell you your coffee cup's on top of the car."

That's the moment I realized that it's not working and something has to change. That the price I was paying wasn't worth it. And that's why today we're going to learn how to break up with stress and take back control of our life with the following strategies.

Did you notice the following?

1. How she painted the picture of chaos by providing the metaphors of both Joan Crawford and the Kardashians?
2. The visual descriptions of the trembling lips and crying eyes?
3. Keep working on your stories to make them shine.

Keep working on your stories to make them shine.

Keep a List of Your Stories

Most of us forget our own stories. I recommend that you keep a running list of your stories open in a Word document, on your smartphone, or in Evernote to jot down a reminder. Even better, create a simple table with the story and then the lesson. You can then easily retrieve and insert them as needed to make a point.

4 Secrets to Great Storytelling

According to the expert in the field and the co-author of *Business Storytelling for Dummies*, Dr. Karen Dietz, there are four key elements needed for any business story to get results. Most people will say you have to have a setting, characters, problem, and resolution. Yawn. Here are the new rules, so try these on for size instead:

1. Find out why the story moves you.

You, as the storyteller, must have an emotional connection to the story. If you understand why the story moves you, you'll be able to move your audience.

2. Share a real experience, not a description.

"I went to the store, I bought some bread, I came home and made a sandwich …" is NOT a story!! It's a list of events—BORING! Share your personal experience and how you were feeling: "I woke up starving and wanted toast for breakfast. But when I opened the fridge, 'Oh, no! No bread!' I hightailed it to the store …"

3. Share the Tension

Every story must have a trouble/struggle to keep us on the edge of our seats. "But when I grabbed the bread and went to check out, I couldn't find my wallet anywhere. OMG, my last $20 was in there!"

4. Have a Key Message

Give us the takeaway from the experience—and at the end, make the invitation. "Well, I learned about the care and feeding of customers…. Maybe next time a customer … you'll be able to take that opportunity to make a difference in someone's life, gain a loyal client, and spark awesome word-of-mouth marketing that builds your business for years to come."

Techniques for Perfecting Your Stories

You need to "sell" your story to the audience; they must hear it and relate to it. Often it means getting the wording and cadence just right. In essence, telling a story is similar to telling a joke: you must give enough information to paint the picture, but not so much information that it overwhelms.

In order to judge the length of a story, I typically tell it into a trusty digital recorder and note the time. If, for example, the story runs six minutes, I'll try it again, aiming for four minutes. It's a delicate balance of getting the mix of time and detail just right.

Another great way to practice your story is to tell it at least five times during the next three days. Bring it up when you are at a networking event, casually weave it into a lunch conversation, or test it on your spouse after work. You're looking to improve upon it each and every time. Be alert for when the story worked and when it bombed. Watch facial expressions and body language. Pay attention to the laughs too; you'll want to allow time for your audience to chuckle so that you don't step on the punch line!

I remember one day buying chocolate bars at IKEA and bringing them home to my son. He said, "Great, Mom, do I have to put those together too?" I repeated the story and it didn't get a laugh. Then I changed the punch line to "Don't tell me: an Allen wrench and assembly required." And they laughed.

Try to paint a picture with your words: tell me about the sights, the sounds, the smells. Act out with your hands the height of a colleague. Show me how you answer the phone or open a jar, etc.

And here's a critical rule: Never tell your audience how they will feel about a story. You can't say, for example, "Here's a funny story." Instead tell the story and see if they laugh.

According to author Carmine Gallo, stories make up 65 to 72 percent of TED talks out of the 500 that he analyzed. And since talks are considered the epitome of excellence, it's clear that stories are the secret to stand-out talks.

WORDS OF LIZDOM

Paint a Picture with Your Stories—
Walk the delicate balance of giving enough information so that the audience can visualize the moment, but not too much information, so that it detracts from your message.

You Are Never the Hero of Your Own Story

I remember listening to an ad executive recall his days of working with Steve Jobs at Apple. He talked about his brilliance, he shared how he saved the day, and he recalled almost single-handedly creating the stunning 1984 commercial. And yet everyone at my table rolled their eyes in exasperation. His talk was all about him!

Even if you are sharing your story, your audience wants to absorb the benefit or result from your experience. Share what you learned and how they can learn too.

Great speakers recognize that you are never the hero of your own story. Why? It makes you look boastful, while at the same time detracting from your message. After all, it's rather difficult to keep tooting your own horn without looking like a one-man brand.

Welcome to the World of The Fictional Truth

My speaking clients often ask me, "What do I do if I am the hero of the story?" Welcome to the world of The Fictional Truth. This galaxy allows you to change characters or places so that someone else is the hero who saves the day. Note that I am not asking you to steal someone else's story or invent a story, but to alter it a little just so that it doesn't reek of vanity.

Sometimes you change a story so as to avoid offending someone. As an example, I tell audiences about my new house and suffering on a 104-degree day without the air conditioning working. Finally, the repairman shows up: a vertically challenged guy who determines the problem in less than two minutes. In a classic Bronx accent, he tells me that the reason my air conditioning isn't working is that I don't have an air conditioner! But I counter that I have a thermostat on the wall, which earns this response: *Aha! Just because you have the right tool doesn't mean you have the right solution to the problem.* As I bring the point of the story home, I share that I too am a Jewish New Yorker. I'm able to mimic the character without offending my tribe. It's an unwritten rule that we can make fun of ourselves but not of others.

In truth, the repairman was Chinese, but the story isn't funny this way. I tried it out on friends and it was viewed as offensive. Voilà! My repairman became Mr. Maury Cooperman!

Liz Goodgold

Tell Universal Stories

A good goal of storytelling is "universality." Talk about things that virtually anyone can relate to: how it still bothers you that your spouse doesn't put the cap back on the toothpaste, for example.

In working with Dr. Annette Conway Marxen, I simply had her share that she was one of very few San Diego natives. This background was especially pertinent, as she was speaking at one of the newest courthouses in our fair city and could share how she remembered her very first trip to court in 1973. It tied into her surroundings and her brand at the same time.

I remember listening to one of my clients in 2008 talk about his just-purchased second home in La Jolla, California. He mentioned how lovely it was going to be to "winter" in San Diego. He was confident that this story made him look good and successful.

Unfortunately, it was my job to tell him the raw truth: with the worst housing recession in over 50 years, most folks in Southern California were just trying to keep one home, let alone buy another! And in these parts, "summer" and "winter" are nouns, not verbs! Telling stories that your audience can't relate to is self-serving; it only makes you feel good while making them feel bad.

As a branding expert, I relay the time in 1976 when I was determined to finally embrace the concept of becoming a California golden girl, just like all of my friends. I went up to the roof of my apartment armed with these essentials: a bottle of Sun-In hair lightener, a small bottle of Johnson & Johnson baby oil, and a glistening silver reflector shield. I sprayed the hair product onto my bright red hair, I oiled my bright white skin, and I held the shield up to my face. For six hours, I baked, I broiled, and I burned.

When I finally returned to our unit, my skin had already begun to blister. My hair was a putrid color of orange, and my face was so hot that my mom thought I was going to die. She opened a jar of

Noxzema with its oddly chemical smell and soothingly applied it to my delicate skin; she then asked the key question of the moment: What was I thinking? I wailed in response that I was just trying to blend in like everybody else. Of course, my mother knew the beauty of branding right then: the goal of branding is to always stand out.

If we dissect this story, you'll observe a good summary about storytelling:

1. I am not the hero of my story; my mother is
2. I use consumer brand names to connect with the audience
3. I use alliterations to boost recall (for example, I baked, I broiled, and I burned)
4. I tell a universal story; most of us can relate to wanting to fit in or getting sunburned
5. I give enough detail to make the story real without causing overwhelm

The Stories Don't All Have to Be Your Stories

Stop worrying that your stories have to be big, amazing, and significant events; they don't! In fact, the stories don't even have to be yours. Retelling how Roger Bannister broke the four-minute mile is inspirational and even teaches us a lesson in perseverance.

WORDS OF LIZDOM

Power of Stories—
Stories teach a lesson, but remember: you are never the hero of your own story. Allow someone else to swoop in to save the day or deliver the key point.

Your only caveat in telling others' stories is to give credit where credit is due. If you share an anecdote from someone else's life, let your audience know. Don't steal other speakers' stories! It frightens me how often I hear others telling my own story about trying to sell Howard Schultz, CEO of Starbucks, quick-bake muffins!

Get Gooder ... Get Going!

1. **Keep a Running List of Your Stories**—Whether it's on Evernote, on your phone, or in Word, the key point is to remember your stories. You can also create a list with one or two shorthand reminders of the story name and then identify the lesson.

2. **Practice Your Story**—Try it out on friends and colleagues. Each time, strive to make it shorter, but richer in meaning and humor.

3. **Time Your Story**—Try it once in the original format, and then see if you can shorten it by at least 20 percent. Tighter stories work better with audiences.

CHAPTER 6

OMG! You Were Awesome!
How to Craft a Killer Talk

It's surprising to me how often presenters forget to stop and identify the key objectives of their talk. Typical objectives include:

- Approve a proposed budget plan
- Demonstrate your credibility
- Sign off on a new idea
- Identify a key problem
- Sell your expertise or services
- Influence opinion
- Boost referrals
- Share a new skill or idea
- Sign up for your coaching program

The First Step in Speechwriting Is
Determining Your Objective

You should have three to five objectives for every talk, but you can't create one word of your speech without first being clear on what you want your audience to know, believe, think, or do. As Ursula Mentjes, bestselling author of *Selling with Intention* and *Selling with Synchronicity,* recommends: "Speak with intention and choose the end result BEFORE you get on stage! SEE that standing ovation! SEE those smiling faces! SEE all of those sales coming in!"

I remember when Richard Dreyfuss called me. As founder of the Dreyfuss Initiative, he is on a mission to change the way social studies is taught in schools. The famed actor explained that he recently gave a talk to hundreds of teachers. "Good," I responded, "but what did you ask them to do? Did you have petitions circulating around the room? Did you sign up volunteers?" He was astounded that he had to tell his audience members what to do. Of course you do! I adore the fact that you can now sign his preamble over at his site. The bottom line is simply this: Arm your audience with the tools necessary to achieve your objectives. If you want them to buy, give them an order form. If you want them to change a law, hand them a petition.

In the 2014 movie *Believe Me*, a character is on the stage ostensibly to raise money for an African charity, and the lead character asks, "Will you give today for a better tomorrow?" As the ushers come through the aisles, he urges the audience to give in a way that reflects their faith. Of course, this "ask" nets an unprecedented amount of donations.

In the Beginning: Don't Write Sentences, Brainstorm Bullets

Most of my speaking clients hit the panic button while looking at a blank screen to craft their talk. They're ready to start writing sentences until I stop them. In speeches, there is never a need to write a complete sentence or paragraph. Bullets are your best friend.

WORDS OF LIZDOM

The Power of Creating Objectives—
Determine the objectives of your talk before writing one word. Then reverse engineer your talk to meet those objectives.

Your first step is to use your screen like a vomitorium—the oft-cited place where Romans used to regurgitate a feast just so they could go back for seconds. In your case, you are just using your PC to quickly spit out all of the talking points in your head. Let each bullet point be a separate thought. Let your fingers fly with examples, stories, lessons, and key points. Go at it for a full 25 minutes without editing your thoughts; go for quantity, not quality.

For the second step, consult your paper files or electronic files for specific companies, case studies, data, or points you want to include. Again, add them as bullets. Wow! You now have tons of content, which leads us to the next step.

Here's another ironic idea that works: try blurting out your thoughts into a digital recorder or even your phone. There are tons of free text-to-speech apps for your phone, including one of my faves, Dragon Dictation. It allows you to speak your thoughts and have them transcribed. Most importantly, it is the key starting point for your outline.

Create an Outline from Your Bullets

Start reviewing your bullets and place them into logical categories, where the content relates to one another. Soon you'll have major buckets of information. In fact, you'll probably have too many buckets. Remember that you are better off conveying three to five key points to your audience rather than ten. Haven't we all encountered a boring speaker? Her time was running out and I bet she was still begging us to stay the course with echoes of "I just have five more points to make." Don't be that type of speaker.

Determine the Order

There are myriad ways to organize the material. Remember: the order doesn't matter, but having an order does! Don't assume that a talk must be presented in chronological order. If, for instance, you were giving a talk on the history of entrepreneurship, you need not start in the 1800s and go forward. You could also organize it starting with today and going backward, highlighting great moments in entrepreneurship. You could also feature three entrepreneurs who changed the face of the industry.

It's All About Them!

Your content should be written from your cynical audiences' point of view. Your audience will be wondering, "Why should I care? What's in it for me?" As a result, your entire content is framed for them. In fact, make sure "you" is rampant through your speech vs. the word "I." As I often say, too many "I's" turns into "Ai yai yai!" Their unspoken questions will be: "Why is your talk important? How can I use this information? How will it help me?"

WORDS OF LIZDOM

**Arm Your Audience with
the Tools to Achieve the Objectives—**
If you want them to buy, give them an order
form; if you want them to change a law,
hand them a petition!

Your talk must therefore solve a problem, highlight an issue, or inspire action. Although you may share a story that happened to you, the reason you always bring it back to the audience is so that they can identify the key lesson. Avoiding self-serving, vanity-laden points is paramount.

At an event for the National Latina Association, I was the morning keynote speaker, and their lunch keynoter was a winner from the TV show *The Apprentice*. She went on and on about Donald Trump's private jet, his hotels, and her celebrity treatment while on the show. The audience was utterly bored. Why? Her entire presentation was about her!

Balance the Content of Your Talk

There's a delicate balance between sharing content, ideas, examples, and inspiration. If you've ever been bored to death with a speaker presenting fact after fact on a PowerPoint, then you'll know that the speaker erred on serving up too much content. Audience members are looking for the speaker to summarize, synthesize, and prioritize the information. You'll hear me say in a speech, "If you only remember one thing …" Or, "If you only make one change to your branding, do …" I am focusing their attention on the critical information.

Less Is More and Less Is Harder than More

As Chris Anderson wrote in the June 2013 issue of the *Harvard Business Review*, "The biggest problem I see in first drafts of presentations is that they try to cover too much ground. You can't summarize an entire career in a single talk." You want to focus your talk on the key objectives. Recognize that giving a shorter talk is harder than giving a longer talk. An 18-minute TED-type talk requires that you practice, rehearse, and nail your timing. There's no room for extraneous detail.

The 16 Goodgold Rules of Speaking Today

Here is the short list of how to create a killer speech today. Every single one of these elements must be incorporated or else you're giving a talk as if it were 1999!

1. Social Media Engagement
2. Humor
3. Interactive Exercise
4. Quantitative Data
5. Fun Factor
6. Stories
7. Emotion
8. Current Event
9. Success Example
10. Flawless-Recall Mechanism
11. Practical Follow-Up Task for Audience
12. Quotable Quote
13. Music
14. Strong Visual Component
15. Kinesthetic Opportunity
16. How to Work, Connect, or Engage with You

Recognizing the preceding essentials, I recommend refining your outline by bolding the major point and then under each major point adding an example, story, fun fact, data point, humorous example, etc., ensuring that your major points are supported. You don't need all 16 Goodgold Rules under each major point, but by the time your talk is complete, every single element should have been incorporated. For a recent talk I gave on branding, here is how my outline looks:

Example of Working
16 Goodgold Rules into a Speech

Major Point: Great Brands Are Consistent

Social Media Engagement
Created the hashtag #brandbetter.

Humor
Told the story of first date with Benjamin with the wire frame glasses. Turns out, his name was Franklin!

Interactive Exercise
Turned to their partner and brainstormed 7-second hook together.

Quantitative Data
We see color within the first five seconds; 98 percent of all marketing communication is sight-based.

Fun Factor
Three folks came to the front and imitated the brands of Paula Deen, Oprah, and Martha Stewart.

Stories
Why no one recognizes me from tennis when I'm dressed for business.

Emotion
How my credit card was denied during the recession for $1.08 at Redbox, and my son breaks down in tears.

Current Event
Relate how Oscar Pistorius being convicted for murder violates his expected brand.

Success Example
Why Nisa Burns of *Kitchenability* always wears her trademark brown chef's coat.

Flawless-Recall Mechanism
Shared Words of Lizdom.

Practical Follow-Up Task for Audience
Gave them the exercise to ask clients, vendors, colleagues, and supervisors to write a list of adjectives.

Quotable Quote
Shared "brand out, stand out, and cash in your business."

Music
Played Marilyn Monroe singing "Happy Birthday" to JFK.

Strong Visual Component
Played 30-second clip of Johnny Cash ("Man in Black") singing at Folsom Prison.

Kinesthetic Opportunity
Participants had to walk around to find a partner who looked like them.

How to Work, Connect, or Engage with You
Shared my order form with all contact info included.

WORDS OF LIZDOM

Less Is More—
You can cover 3–5 main points
in a speech; that's it! The power is recognizing
that less is more powerful and memorable.

Compare the Outline to the Objectives

This is where the rubber meets the road in terms of speaking. You want to review your list of objectives and compare it to your outline. If your goal was to influence the committee to sign your recommended budget, have you provided enough facts to make your case? Are there enough data points to prove the positive return on investment that you've proposed? Are all your examples relevant enough to build your case? If not, go back and add more information so that by just the outline alone, you are achieving your objective.

How to Start a Speech the Right Way

If you do an online search for "starting a speech," you'll find, as I did, that at the top of the results is asking a question, telling a joke, or quoting somebody else. All of these are wrong! Read on as to why these speech starters are nonstarters. Here are my Seven Deadly Sins of Starting a Speech.

Seven Deadly Sins of Starting a Speech

Deadly Sin #1: Starting Your Speech with a Question

When you start your talk with a question, you confuse the audience. Imagine that I have just taken the stage and asked, "How many of you want to make more money?" You're confused, because you don't know if you're supposed to answer, raise your hand, shout out a response, or if the question is merely rhetorical. Lesson: Never ask a rhetorical question in a speech!

You're also a little bewildered, because it's such an ignorant question. Of course virtually everyone wants to make more money! Duh! These types of questions just insult your audience.

Let me be clear: I am NOT saying don't ask your audience questions. You can do it later in your talk, as long as you are crystal clear that you want them to answer. Raise your hand yourself if you want them to raise their hands. Ask your question this way: "By a show of hands, let me …" Or use gestures if you want them to shout it out. Cup your hand against your ear. See my YouTube channel (Liz Goodgold) for a segment entitled "Effectively Using Hand Gestures While Speaking."

Deadly Sin #2: Starting Your Speech with a Quote

Here's the quickest way for your audience to believe you're pompous: start with a quote. No matter who you quote, from Eleanor Roosevelt to Bill Cosby, someone will tune you out. It just reeks of trying too hard.

Deadly Sin #3: Starting Your Speech with a Definition

Can you say boring? This method is not just low-key, it's off key! We didn't come to a talk on leadership to hear the dictionary definition of the word.

Deadly Sin #4: Starting Your Speech with Housekeeping Issues

This sin is repeatedly committed in webinars and seminars. Presenters start late, telling the crowd that they are waiting for all to join, and then explain how long they're going to talk, the location of the restrooms, and other minutiae. No! Grab their attention and then later, perhaps 15 minutes in, mention these issues.

Deadly Sin #5: Trying to Teach a Lesson

Speaking today isn't a lesson: you don't teach and your audience doesn't learn. As adults, we quest for more knowledge, but we want to discover, explore, uncover, or understand—not "learn." Presenting your material like a history lesson or a schoolteacher just puts us squarely back in 7th grade with the typical memories of dread and boredom.

Deadly Sin #6: Starting Your Speech with a Data Dump

We assume that you know your topic. After all, that's why you have the floor. So don't bury us deep in data. Data is important, but it's impersonal and defeats the main goal of starting a speech, which is letting us get to know you. So, just as I highlighted in the Goodgold Rules of Speaking, leave the quantitative portion for later in your program.

Deadly Sin #7: Starting Your Speech with a Joke

Two nuns walk into a bar … stop me if you've heard this one. We are presenters, entrepreneurs, executives, coaches, employees, and keynote speakers. We are not comedians. As a result, we cannot tell jokes per se. We *can* make our audience laugh, but we do it with stories and observations. Leave formal joke telling to the late-night talk show hosts.

Start Your Speech Slow and Build

Yikes! Now that I've shared the wrong ways to start a speech, you're probably wondering what are the right ways to start a speech. I'll give you a variety of options below, but keep this contrarian point of view in mind: I want you to start low-key. Really! Yes, the opening is critical, but if you start on a really high note, there is only one way to go from there—down. You don't want that!

Further, the goal of starting a speech is to give the audience a chance to get to know you; they're observing, listening, and recognizing your voice, your cadence, and your gestures. Let them learn to like you so that they can eventually fall in love with you.

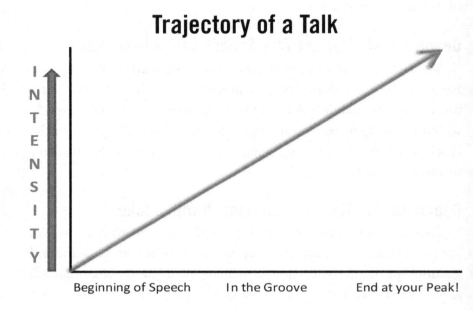

Trajectory of a Talk

WORDS OF LIZDOM

Start Your Speech on a Low Note—
Start your talk very low-key;
if you start spectacularly, there is
no place to go but down.

How to Start a Speech the Right Way

Here are a few practical ideas for starting your talk in a low-key way.

Personal Story

A personal story that is relevant always works. (See chapter 5 for more information on storytelling.) Share about getting there that day, talk about how you are like them, open up about your troubled times. The goal is to share something that is authentically you.

Startling Statistic

Do you know that 47 percent of American girls in second grade don't eat lunch because they're afraid of getting fat? Did I grab your attention? Can you see how one startling statistic such as this one allows my client, Kym Piekunka, author of *A Sister Weighs In*, to speak poignantly about body image?

Big Tease

Steve Jobs was the master in teasing his audience about what's coming next with his product launches. He sets up a major introduction, he explains that it's going to revolutionize the world … and then bam! Out comes the iPhone.

Full Frontal

I call this approach "What you see is what you get" because it's a simple, strong, direct opening: "I'm going to introduce you to the best sales technique you've never heard of before."

Great Example

In this case, the story doesn't have to be yours. It can be pulled from the media. Just as long as it is relevant and interesting, it works.

Visual Prop

I've taken to the stage with an enormous robin's egg blue box tied with an exquisite bow. Virtually none of the audience can see the brand name (Tiffany) written on the box, but almost everyone, especially women, recognizes the brand just from its color. In short, it's a great prop to introduce the power of color branding.

Video Clip

With over 100 hours of video clips uploaded every single minute to YouTube, no speaker is without extraordinary resources to make a relevant point.

Audio Clip

Sound is a powerful tool; I have played the audio of James Earl Jones saying, "This is CNN," and then played the voice of Fran Drescher to demonstrate the power of the voice. It grabs attention.

WORDS OF LIZDOM

Rip an Example from the Headlines—
To show your audience that your speech is current and relevant, always pull an item from the past week's news.

Never Introduce Your Introduction

A common problem I see at the beginning of a speech is introducing your introduction. In other words, you say, "I'm going to start today by ..." NO! Just start! Or, "Let me tell you a funny story." You don't get to tell us that the story is funny. Tell it and we'll let you know.

Giving Body to Your Body of the Talk

This is the meat of your talk; this is what people came to hear. Refer to your outline and present the material, sprinkling it liberally with stories, examples, case studies, facts, music, interactive exercises, humor, emotion, kinesthetic exercises, and news ripped from the headlines so that you are interesting. Keep comparing your material to your objective to ensure that you stay on point.

Concluding the Talk

People tend to remember the first piece of information and the last piece. Restaurants have mastered this concept and therefore put the most appetizing and profitable items at the top and the bottom of the menu, knowing that as we skim the menu, we'll remember what's at the beginning and the end, and forget what's in the middle. I call creating your speech with the important stuff at the top and bottom the "Sandwich Effect": the bologna is always in the middle. So make sure you end your talk on the highest note.

Brand-new rules demand that we avoid ending with a summary. Ugh! That ending is so 1999. We conclude with a call to action, a question to ponder, a killer story, or an emotional example. But remember: we never utter the phrase "in conclusion." Why? Because it signals to the audience that you are coming to an end, and they immediately tune out.

Get Gooder ... Get Going!

1. **Create Your Speech Objectives**—Every single talk requires that you create three to five goals of the talk. If you don't know the end goal, it's impossible to reach it.

2. **Brainstorm All Potential Points of Your Talk**—Quickly brainstorm for at least 25 minutes, striving for quantity, not quality. Put each thought in its own bullet point.

3. **Include the 16 Goodgold Rules in Your Talk**—If it's easier, color code your outline so you can easily see what's missing.

4. **Cull the Media for a Timely Tie-in**—To ensure that your talk is relevant, intentionally pluck a news item from the week and find an appropriate home for it in your talk.

CHAPTER 7

Preparation of H:
How to Plan for the Unexpected

Nothing ever goes as planned. It's just a fact of speaking ... and life too! You can't control the unexpected, but you can control *how* you deal with it. The most important item to remember is the mantra from the movie *Frozen*: Let it go! If you are flustered, the audience will feel flustered. If you're nervous, they will feel your nerves. You need to let unplanned surprises roll off your back just like water off a duck.

In my speaking career, every possible calamity has occurred: fire, earthquake, roof leaking onto my head, twisting my ankle, and many other oddities. When I was keynoting at the Women in Business event in 2001, my lavalier microphone literally sparked and caught fire! Throughout the entire episode, I joked with my audience—wanting them to feel comfortable even though I was inwardly panicked. Corny jokes spewed from my mouth, such as, "I told you I was hot; in fact, I'm on fire!"

When an earthquake rocked the room during a speech in Riverside, California, I laughed it off with, "You gotta shake things up with branding." At a 2014 event, I literally walked out of my shoes—twice! (Yep, there was an uneven grate on the stage and my heel kept getting caught.) On this occasion, my refrain was, "I said I was gonna knock your socks off, but I didn't tell you I was going to knock my *own* shoes off!" Clearly, having a sense of humor saves the day.

Humorist Karyn Buxman literally walked off the stage and fell flat on her back into the orchestra pit at a San Francisco gig. After catching her breath, bolting upright, and reclaiming the microphone, she uttered: "And now I'll take questions from the floor!" The audience loved her and laughed with her, not at her.

When dealing with an unexpected occurrence, my priority, of course, is making sure everyone is safe; but after that, you have to be willing to stay in the moment—even if you're uncomfortable or thrown off your game momentarily. The worst thing to do is to pretend nothing has happened. If you've lost your place in your speech and can't seem to get a handle on where you've been, try asking your audience. A simple request such as "Where were we again?" should work. You audience wants you to succeed and will step in to help.

The worst option is to pretend nothing has happened and ignore it. Your audience sees it; your audience knows it. You must address it head-on and then keep going.

Be Prepared

If the first rule of thumb is to let it go, the second rule also comes from a Disney movie. As Scar in *The Lion King* so aptly sings: Be Prepared. No, you never know what will happen, but you can prepare for the unexpected. Aways have these essentials with you:

Wardrobe Essentials

1. Extra shirt
2. Second tie
3. Spare pair of stockings

4. Safety pins
5. Complete spare outfit if checking a bag. Always assume the airlines will lose your luggage, so carry on everything you need

Logistical Essentials

- Exact directions (double-check Google Maps!)
- Parking information (critical if speaking on the campus of a large university or company)
- Emergency cell phone number of at least two staff members who are organizing the event
- Admittance Info (do you need a badge?)
- Hotel confirmation number (if staying the night)
- Cocktail party info
- Transportation info (how are you getting to the party?)

Business Essentials

Name Tag

As we discussed in chapter 3, I recommend having your own magnetic name tag and taking it with you to all speaking events.

Business Cards

Never leave home without these!

Verbal Introduction

Even though you have emailed it in advance, assume your announcer has lost or misplaced it. Please print out in large font so that anyone can read it *without* glasses!

Spare Batteries

This little item will save you tons of aggravation when your pointer, digital recorder, or remote runs out of juice.

Office Supplies

Scissors, tape, pens, whiteboard markers, stapler, binder clips, and rubber bands to organize paper and information.

Rope/CSI Crime Scene Tape

For roping off seats; see chapter 8 for more information on controlling your environment.

Raffle Bowl

I use a bright red acrylic one that works with my brand and my breakable life. Other speakers use martini glasses, fishbowls, etc.

Blank Raffle Forms

Just in case your audience doesn't have or didn't bring business cards. Raffles are explained more in chapter 14.

Raffle Gift

Try to find a brand-appropriate gift; more information on conducting the raffle is covered in detail in chapter 14.

Battery Booster/Charger

Sometimes all you need is just a little more juice to power your iPhone, Android, or iPad when you can't get to a charging station.

Point-of-Sale Materials

You can't make the sale if you don't have the tools; make sure to have your order form, special offers, credit card machine, or mobile method for accepting credit cards (Square, PayPal, Intuit, etc.).

Props

Items you use to boost the fun factor (for example, Red Fireballs, flash cards, deck of cards, etc.).

Items for Sale

Books, CDs, downloads, etc.

Tablecloth

Never assume a table comes with a tablecloth. Get one in a brand-appropriate color if you don't have a special one created.

It's All About Them, Not You

To truly succeed in speaking gooder, your talks must be customized to your audience. Giving the same talk over and over without regard to who is in the audience is a flagrant sign of disrespect.

Knowing the Audience Means Asking Questions

In order to prepare for a killer presentation, ask the meeting planner, organizer, or even your boss a minimum of these questions. I also arm all of my coaching clients with a much longer list to ensure that their talk resonates with the audience.

1. How many attendees will be there?
2. What percentage of men/women will there be?
3. Is this meeting mandatory?
4. What's the purpose of the conference?
5. Is there a theme?
6. Will any spouses be in attendance?
7. What position do the attendees hold?

8. What companies or industries are represented?
9. Can you get a list of the attendees and/or company list so that you can review their websites in advance?
10. Is there a regional slant to the conference?
11. Will any VIPs be in the audience?
12. Is any individual or company being recognized for special achievement?
13. Are there any topics to avoid like the plague?
14. Is there a running inside joke?

How to Ask Better Questions to Understand Your Audience Better

One of the surprising facts I discovered in my speaking career was how often I was unintentionally led astray by a meeting planner. I would be told, for instance, that my audience was packed with C-level executives, only to discover that virtually all of my attendees were mid- or low-level managers. Or, that my audience was well versed in internal branding, but when I went into the topic, I was met with blank faces. Let's be clear: no one needs to truly understand the audience better than you! To evaluate your audience, I've developed these tools:

WORDS OF LIZDOM

Don't Assume—
Don't assume that the meeting organizer has all of the answers about the audience. Test your assumptions by actually talking to upcoming attendees and asking questions directly.

Ask to Interview Three to Five Confirmed Attendees

I recall being booked as a keynote speaker for the National Association of Electrical Distributors. Since this was a specialized industry of which I knew nothing, I requested to speak to a few of their confirmed attendees. Here are a few questions I asked:

1. What is the number-one issue facing your industry?
2. What is your biggest marketing obstacle?
3. Is the industry encountering any major changes?
4. How is technology impacting your work?
5. If you could find the answer to one big marketing question, what would it be?
6. What's your top goal in attending the conference?
7. What one or two items do you most want to discover?
8. If you attended the conference in the past, what made it a success?
9. What are your key likes/dislikes regarding your past speakers?

Request Industry Publications

Even with the web, it's hard to take a deep dive into an industry, because so often its key content is behind a paywall. By requesting the group's publications, you get an insider's view: seeing who is advertising, noting the giants of the industry, discovering the issues, and realizing future challenges.

Go Beyond the Website

Of course, I expect you to visit the organization or company website, but you can do more online research as well. Visit member sites, connect with folks via LinkedIn, check out the recent tweets, "like" relevant sites on Facebook so that you get their feed. Don't forget to take the pulse of the industry by seeing the chatter online via reviews, Yelp, Angie's list, and other rating sites. Forewarned is forearmed.

Always Attend the Cocktail Party or Opening Session

I'll often hear from top-rated speakers that they simply swoop in to give their talk and then fly away immediately afterward. My advice: arrange your schedule to attend both the opening session and the cocktail party. It yields amazing opportunities on many fronts.

Firstly, informal networking gives you the chance to meet audience members. No longer will you be speaking to strangers, but to friends. Additionally, you get to mingle with real guests, ensuring that your talk is on point and on target. Thirdly, you can even add examples directly from this audience, making your talk even more relevant. When I was booked to speak for the National Council of Postal Credit Unions, I learned that two of the credit unions had just changed their names. Before the morning's talk, I was able to easily add these examples right into my presentation.

Listening to the opening remarks lets you know what's being said and emphasized. Have you ever been to a talk and realized that the previous speaker just said the exact same thing? You can't control what someone else says, but you can control and adapt your talk based on what you hear.

The final reason for mingling is that the best source for booking more speeches is from someone who has just heard you speak. Developing contacts at the event allows you to follow up and scour for additional speaking opportunities.

Plan to Stay After Your Presentation

Whether you're talking to college students, colleagues, or your peers, allot time to linger. In other words, get there early and stay late. Don't schedule events immediately following your presentation. The interaction afterward is typically when the amazing opportunities appear.

Get There Early and Greet Your Audience

Every time you give a speech, get there early. It not only allows you to set up the room, but also to talk to audience members. In shaking hands at my event for the North San Diego Business Chamber on how to give a talk, I thought my audience would be all entrepreneurs. It turned out that they were all employees who needed to speak better in order to get promoted. Whew! Glad I asked!

Survey Your Attendees

Another way to determine your audience's needs is to ask them! In preparation for a webinar for Meals on Wheels, for example, I was able to ask two questions automatically via their site's registration link. It gave me time to tailor the talk while at the same time making my presentation spot-on!

Tailor Stories for Different Audiences

Different stories work for different audiences. I share more about my poverty-stricken upbringing with female audiences than with male ones. If I have a preponderance of males, I'm sure to include examples from sports, politics, and gender-neutral brands. If I have a young audience, I avoid examples that occurred before their time, or what I call the "pre-Elizabethan" era. I remember sharing a joke about Jim Croce with a class at the University of San Diego, only to discover that not one single student knew who the singer was!

I'm now super sensitive to religious preferences as well. Why? Because I truly stepped in it during a speech in Tulsa, Oklahoma. I tripped off the stage and broke my ankle. Unfortunately, for many female members of the Bible Belt, I uttered, "Oh, God." Despite six hours of a great all-day seminar, the number-one comment to the meeting planner was how I took the Lord's name in vain.

Taking my hard-learned lesson to heart, I altered my presentation for a keynote talk in Pocatello, Idaho, which, like Utah, has a large Mormon population. I avoided any wine jokes and changed my handout from the 10 Commandments of Branding to the Top 10 Rules of Branding lest I offend my audience.

WORDS OF LIZDOM

Always Show Up to Your Event Extremely Early—
Showing up early takes away stress from the meeting organizer and allows you to breathe easy. Allow extra time for traffic, getting lost, or parking issues.

Get Gooder ... Get Going!

1. **Understand Your Audience**—Speak to potential attendees, ask questions in advance, request industry publications, send out a questionnaire, google company representatives, and check out LinkedIn for attendee bios.

2. **Plan on Arriving Early and Staying Late**—Don't schedule an event immediately after the event. Allow time to interact and speak with attendees.

3. **Budget Time to Attendthe Cocktail Party and Opening Address**—Listen to the conversation informally at the event and be sure to remain attentive to the talks before your presentation; it is always worth the effort.

4. **Prepare Your Emergency Kit**—Have your wardrobe, business, and speech essentials with you just in case of emergency.

CHAPTER 8

A Room With a View:
Setting Up Your Room for Success

If speaking is all about the experience, then controlling your entire environment is critical. In 2000 I was speaking in Boston and I knew I had the crowd in the palm of my hand—they were listening, they were learning, and they were laughing. Yet the evaluations were only mediocre. Why? The number-one complaint was about the temperature of the room. Really!!

By the end of this chapter, you'll know how to control your environment so that you earn the raves, rewards, and recognition you deserve.

Bring an Assistant, Colleague, Intern, or Mom to Help

My first piece of advice is to bring an assistant with you to all of your presentations. You can invite colleagues, interns, or even someone who wants to work with you. It becomes a great win-win: They get to attend for free, and you get the help you need. If these options fail, arrange for someone at the event to be your helper. In my case, my favorite helper is my mom. My great Jewish mother is the one who can sweet-talk the organizer into anything. She acts as usher, greeter, escort, and even queen of back-of-the-room sales.

Create the Setting for Good Energy

Since virtually all attendees gravitate toward taking a seat at the back of a meeting room, your job (Mr. Phelps) is to get them to sit toward the front and sit close together. Having a large room with scattered participants throughout tends to suck the energy out of the room. Sitting close together fosters interaction and even makes the laughter more contagious. And if you are doing any videotaping (essential for your YouTube channel), showing a half-empty rooms brands you as a failure.

Think back to when you last went out to the movies and laughed your guts out. Compare that with watching a movie by yourself. Did you notice that sharing the experience with others makes it better and "funner"?

Fill the Room the Way You Want It

If you want your audience seated close together at the front, make it happen. A key preemptive strike is to include your preferred room setup needs on your website or in a follow-up confirming email. You can find my list of room setup items over at www.refirebranding.com.

In the interim, however, here are a few tricks:

1. Have your helper act as an usher
Escort guests to a seat while simultaneously giving them a handout.

2. Rope off the back few rows
Have fun with this idea, even using CSI yellow crime scene tape as a fun factor. Or simply use rope, but remember to add this item to your traveling speaker's kit, mentioned in chapter 7.

3. Take away all extra chairs

You've now created a high-stakes game of musical chairs. There are only enough chairs for the folks in attendance, forcing them to sit close together.

4. Fold down the extra chair

If it's physically impossible to remove the extra chairs, turn the backs down, signifying that they are off limits.

5. Place reserved signs on chairs or faraway tables

Most people respect a "reserved" sign, so this solution works rather well.

6. Only put handouts on the front chairs

Aha! Perhaps this one will work for you.

7. Place special treats on the first few rows

You'd be surprised how a little something special entices the curious to choose those seats.

8. Rearrange the rows such that the seats are always in an even number.

In that manner, you can easily conduct the essential interactive exercises when you say, "Turn to your neighbor."

WORDS OF LIZDOM

Own Your Environment—
Whether it is your own sponsored event or you are the speaker at an event, you control the environment. Take control to make it work for you!

Act Like a Banquet Manager

Whether it is my own hosted event or not, I take a critical look at everything affecting my attendees.

- Temperature of the room—Can it be easily adjusted? If so, who can you contact?
- Brightness of the Room—You need the audience to see and almost feel your facial movements. So turn the lights up so that they can see every gesture.
- Restrooms—Are there enough of them? Just a few months ago, the wonderful organizers of the Women's Business Conference in Anaheim recognized that with 500 ladies in attendance, restrooms were at a premium. What did they do? They created signs and turned the men's units into women's bathrooms! Pure genius!
- Food and Beverages—I am a firm believer in the power of caffeine and provide copious amounts of great coffee. I also believe in good nutrition, so my signature item for breakfast seminars is hard-boiled eggs; it's low calorie, high protein, and easy to bring to any event.
- Name Tags—Are name tags easy to access? Names foster interaction and connection.
- Wi-Fi—Since we know that iPads and phones won't be turned off, you might as well post the Wi-Fi code and Twitter hashtag on a whiteboard to facilitate the sharing of information.
- Test the room for "dead spots" with the microphone—Many ballrooms have low ceilings, which create a killer echo. Others have places where the microphone doesn't even work! Test the room with a working microphone to know in advance.

Dealing with Technology

I am one of the few speakers who speak without notes or PowerPoint, but I'm sensitive to others who do use visual aids. Let me just say that this area is fraught with danger. Here's how to reduce technical glitches:

1. Carry Your Presentation in Many Different Forms and Formats

Just to be for sure, for sure, I would email myself my presentation, send it to the organizer, carry it on a flash drive, have it on my PC, and even store it on my phone or iPad. I would also have it in PowerPoint and as a PDF.

2. Travel with Your Own Equipment

If the "pointer" or PPT is crucial to your success, bring it with you! Have spare VGA connectors, your PC, and your projector all assembled and ready to wheel to your event.

3. Have a Backup

If ALL of your technology fails, can you still give your presentation? Make sure you can!

WORDS OF LIZDOM

**Act Like
You Own the Joint!**
It's better to beg for forgiveness
than ask for permission.

Avoiding Handout Chaos

Handouts help reinforce your brand name and provide crucial contact information. Therefore, include your email, social media handles, and phone number on every single page. I've seen tons of handouts where only the website is included. Big mistake; it assumes that readers will click on over to your site. If you do this, you are simply hoping or praying that they will connect with you. Please also number your pages just in case the pages get separated. And don't forget this gem: leave lots of white space so that listeners can take copious notes. My rule of thumb is that high-end, highly paid speeches deserve content-rich handouts. Clearly, then, pro bono speeches get simple one-pagers, but with lots of essential white space.

I like fill-in-the-blank handouts. However, they require that you guide your attendees through filling out *all* the blanks. If you run long and don't get to the entire handout, your participants will feel cheated. Moreover, you'll undoubtedly have a few stragglers asking for the "answer" way back on item #1. To solve this dilemma, I suggest you post a completed handout on your website and note that URL at the end of your handout for easy reference.

A few coaches suggest that you eschew handouts altogether and allow your participants to write what they hear as noteworthy. This method allows you maximum flexibility, but it also deprives them of a clear "takeaway." Other experts recommend distributing a handout at the end so that the audience has followed you for the entire journey and they now have a solid reference point. My suggestion is to try a few different methods to see what suits you best.

If you choose to create a handout, you can distribute it right before your presentation. Again, this is where your "helper" comes in. (See chapter 7 under "Be Prepared.") Another option is to have forwarded your materials to the meeting planner in advance so that they are all included in the booklet distributed at the start of the conference.

Whichever method you use to distribute a handout, ensure that you use it. In other words, keep the audience focused on where you are. Here's an example from one of my speeches demonstrating how I keep the audience following along with the handout: "'Speak like your peeps' is a good rule of thumb when describing your business. Don't use *your* words; use the words people in your industry use. And that's the key point of page two. At the top of page two, let's all fill in the blank with 'Speak like your peeps.'"

Since I'm such a believer in the digital world, I like to electronically send a follow-up email with key points and other value takeaways. This technique is really good for sending links, reference lists, as well as other items that are long and cumbersome on a printed page, but easily presented as a hot link.

As you know by now, I rarely use PowerPoint, and if I did, I think sending your slides to attendees is a no-win situation. Here's why: it allows audiences to more easily "steal" your intellectual property, it prevents any meaningful follow-up, and it simply rehashes what you wrote, not what you said.

The bottom line on electronic follow-up is that it gives you a reason to remain connected with your audience. And your meaty follow-up is a solid reason why participants willingly give you their email address.

WORDS OF LIZDOM

Handouts Can Help or Hurt—
Determine your preferred method of handouts—bullets or fill-in-the blank— but have them easy to read and easily available at your talk.

Get Gooder ... Get Going!

1. **Get a Helper**—Three weeks in advance, snag a colleague or administrative assistant to help you with the back of the room.

2. **Create a Seating Plan**—Determine your device for discouraging sitting at the back of the room.

3. **Develop a Handout Template**—Have a branded template at the ready for all of your events. Make sure it is well designed, easy to read, has all of your contact information, and plenty of white space for notes.

CHAPTER 9

How to Craft Sexy Speaking Titles and Downright Delicious Descriptions

L et me be abundantly clear: We are all selling our talks. Even as an employee, you are "selling" your talk to the CEO, to the circulation list on the invitation, and to your colleagues.

Titles Sell Everything

It is the title of your talk that sells you to the meeting planner; it is the title that gets butts in seats; it is the title that gets people to pay to attend your talk. Your title should be so exciting that men and women are jumping up and down, ready to throw money at you to hear what you have to say!

Titles must be sexy and sizzling; they need to have high energy and high imagery. The goal for a speaking title is exactly the same as for a book: get the reader to say, "Yes! I want that." Here's a title I respect: *Make Him Beg to Be Your Boyfriend in 6 Simple Steps,* by Michael Fiore.

Titles Must Promise a Benefit, Result, or Experience

One of my clients is a health insurance agent. She was thrilled for the opportunity to present at the local chamber of commerce, since it was a good business-building opportunity. Her title? Health Insurance 101. Do you think that would fill a room? I don't. We changed it to *Preventing Health Insurance Headaches: 6 Easy Steps for Selecting a Quality Carrier.*

Always think in terms of what benefit or result your talk will provide your audience. Your talk is always about them! After they hear you speaking, they'll understand how to make healthy food choices, master social media, or focus more effectively. Your audience doesn't want to know that the task is arduous, painful, difficult, long, or hard. There's a reason why diet books that promise to lose a dress size in a week sell better than books telling you that it is a long, hard, slow process!

Remember that your title doesn't ask a question, but answers it. For example, one of my clients created this proposed title: "Can You Double Your Impact by Leveraging Your Style?" See how much better it sounds as "4 Stunning Ways to Wow Your Team, Deepen Relationships, and Skyrocket Your Impact."

I remember working with Tedde McMillen, the co-founder of the Oregon Chai Tea Company, which she later sold for $75 million. After she wrote her book about the journey, she was promoting herself as a speaker, but her titles weren't selling. Notice how her "before" titles were merely labels; they lacked the sizzle. Take a look at the revised results.

Before	After with a Little Lizdom
The History of Tea	Steeped in Tradition: Quirky Facts, Amazing Stories, and The Art of Making Tea
How to Create a Food Product	The Magic Recipe for Success: How to Turn Your Idea Into a Multimillion-Dollar Business
How to Succeed as a Woman Business Owner	The Strained Life: The Secrets to Overcoming Fear, Failure, and Fraud to Succeed as a Woman Business Owner

A Beginning Formula of Titles

In order to get you started, I created the magic formula below based upon speeches that routinely sell out. You start with your number of steps, processes, or formulas; add an adjective; layer in the key formula, and then add the result. Watch:

Number	Adjective	Collective Noun	Preposition	Benefit/Result
6	Simple	Secrets	to	Making Healthy Food Choices
7	Easy	Rules	for	Mastering Social Media
22	Fast	Formulas	to	Focus More Effectively
941	Quick	Steps	for	Organizing Any Room

WORDS OF LIZDOM

Titles Must Sell—
Titles are essential for speaking success. They must promise a benefit, result, or experience.

Layering Nuance Appeal to Your Title

If the preceding formula was your first step, we can now embellish it with other techniques. Notice that if the first part of the title is the sizzle, the second part sells the steak (meaning the benefit or result).

Sex Appeal

Look how even math becomes hot with a variation of the bestseller *The Joy of Sex* with: *The Joy of x: A Guided Tour of Math, from One to Infinity,* or this book title: Look Better Naked.

Your Brand DNA

Clearly you know that I love to play with words, so of course I could create this speech title: *6 Simple Ways to Make Speeches Funner.* If I can share how to speaker gooder, why wouldn't I be able to make this exercise funner? Get it?

Alliterations

Alliterations are simply when the first sounds of a word are the same. In the case of brand names, you have Coca-Cola, Constant Contact, Weight Watchers, and Cap'n Crunch. I worked with Phyllis Pearson on her book and you can see alliterations at work in the subtitle: *A Taste to Remember: Retro Recipes Revised for Gluten-Free Living.*

Rhymes

Rhymes are the fastest way to boost recall. *How to go from break-up to make-up: 5 strategies for mending your relationship.*

Humor

Get us laughing and you'll have quickly roped in your audience. I adore *Woe Is I* by Patricia T. O'Conner.

Opposites

This is a time-tested strategy that still works for Target's tagline: Expect More, Pay Less. Or, as in Steve Harvey's book *Act Like a Lady, Think Like a Man* or Dr. Connell Cowan and Dr. Melvyn Kinder's *Smart Women/Foolish Choices*. Dr. Lois Frankel has a variation of this theme with *Why Men Are Heard and Women Are Liked: **Capitalizing on Communication Differences in the Workplace.***

WORDS OF LIZDOM

Fish Don't See Water—
It's often hard to take an objective view of ourselves and our titles. Ask for an outside opinion so that you can create a title that works.

Of course, writing titles forces you to take a step back from your topic and look at the field objectively. As I like to say, "Fish don't see water," so this objective view is hard. It's also the primary reason why my clients hire me: to provide insight plus creativity to create both book and speaking titles that sell.

Get Gooder ... Get Going!

1. **Understand the Benefit or Result That You Are Selling—** Before creating your title, make sure you understand the clear benefit and write it down in a full-frontal way.

2. **Convert Your Boring Titles into Sexy Speaking Titles**—Now, convert your titles using the provided formulas; use numbers, easy, simple, and alliterations to add interest and recall.

CHAPTER 10

Red-Hot Secrets for Writing Bios and Verbal Introductions

There is a huge difference between a résumé and a bio. Whereas a résumé is the standard chronological listing of your jobs, a bio links it all together to sell the brand YOU! Red-hot bios make it clear what position you are in, your credibility, your responsibility, and how you serve others in that role.

Why You Need a Bio

Your bio should be an easy-to-read document broken up with tons of headers, fostering my assertion that we are all stricken with ADD: too much work and not enough time. These headers allow the reader to skim your bio and pick up the highlights. Once you have your bio written, there are a host of places you will want to use it. It belongs on your LinkedIn profile, as a stand-alone PDF document to send to others to get hired, as an essential piece of your speaker's package, and as a starting point for creating your verbal introduction. This document, of course, also belongs on your website or the company website where thumbnail profiles are displayed. You can see many examples of before and after bios by simply heading over to www.speakgooder.com/bonus and entering the code BONU$.

How to Write a Killer Bio in 5 Easy Steps

Do you see that the preceding header is a model of writing a sexy title? A biography often stumps the writer, because in this case, the writer and the subject are the same! In other words, it's hard to write about you!

Step 1: Connect the Dots

The biggest mistakes I see in biographies are laundry lists of disparate jobs that make the reader scratch her head and think, "Huh?" Your job is to link all of the information together to show how it has made you a better you! One of my clients, Dawn Fleming, was ready to dismiss her legal career as irrelevant when she launched her entrepreneurial venture. Yet, when you read the sentence below, you can clearly see how it adds value: *Since many businesses find themselves in legal trouble that could have been avoided with sound legal counsel, Dawn utilizes her Juris Doctor within a business context.*

When explaining how Dr. Arden Bercovitz impersonates Dr. Albert Einstein in his Einstein Alive presentations, I connected it this way: *"Dr. Bercovitz captures the essence of Dr. Einstein because he too studied physics. He received his PhD in Reproductive Endocrinology from the University of Missouri, Columbia, his MS from the University of Washington, Pullman, and his BS from Cal Poly, Pomona."*

Step 2: Demonstrate Credibility

Credibility can be demonstrated in many different ways, including these:

- Number of years in the position
- Current title
- Awards won
- Press appearances
- Name of prestigious school or university
- Studied under major authority
- Contests won
- PR appearances

- Books written
- Client list
- Writing credentials
- Number of followers on Twitter
- Number of likes on Facebook
- Youngest/oldest/first to achieve something
- Innovative ideas or products

Step 3: Name-Drop to Boost Your Reputation

Co-branding merely means using another brand to boost your own. It's commonplace in the consumer products world. For example, when I was at Quaker Oats, Nestlé boasted that its Toll House oatmeal cookies were made with real Quaker Oats.

To adapt this concept to your bio, you want to profile your "brand name" experience. Instead of writing "10 years of experience with a top advertising agency," change it to "10 years with Wieden+Kennedy." If you worked for 15 years for Merck or Pfizer, add it!

Step 4: Add a "Cool" Quotient

Do you remember hearing résumé writers tell you to delete anything personal from your résumé, such as the "Interests" section? Well, they're wrong! Every single time I write a bio, I always add a quirky fact. One of my workshop attendees was reluctant to mention that she is a former Laker Girl, but since she added it, it's become the lead conversation starter. Another client, Miffy Weller-Jones, boasts on her bio that she produced three TV ads while at Nike with Michael Jordan. This accomplishment has both the cool quotient and the co-branding working for her! Another workshop attendee was embarrassed to mention that he wrestled in the Olympics because he didn't medal. Who cares? His Olympics experience demonstrates strength and tenacity. It's a great cool quotient!

Chief Mind Officer Christian Wasinger incorporates this cool quotient and ties it back into his core competency: Apropos for a dancer, Christian is also quick on his feet in addressing questions, providing interactive exercises, and boosting audience participation. Even my husband, Patrick Pieper, has a de facto interesting fact: he's one of ten children!

Step 5: Add a Benefit or Results Statement

You don't merely want to list your experience, but also boast how it will help others. My bio below, for instance, states: *Her specialized, one-on-one branding and coaching programs typically lift her clients' income by 40%!*

Author Henry DeVries' bio includes this sentence: *Henry speaks to thousands of marketers each year, teaching them new ways to maximize revenues and increase lead generation results.*

WORDS OF LIZDOM

There Is a Difference Between a Bio and an Intro— A written bio is for the eyes; a verbal introduction is for the ears.

6 Keys to Writing a Verbal Introduction

You never want to chance letting someone else introduce you without a prepared verbal introduction. It's the quick-start way to fail. After all, you are the expert on you!

You also don't want to make the mistake of handing someone your bio before you take center stage. Instead, hand them a custom-created verbal introduction intended to be read aloud. Few speakers create an intro, but it's critical in preparing the audience for your presentation. An intro is different from a bio because it's written clearer and shorter; the brain processes information differently when it's read rather than heard.

1. Write in short sentences

A good introduction is short with strong, punchy sentences. It cannot run longer than 60 seconds when read aloud. Test your final draft before delivering it.

2. Eliminate long, compound sentences

These types of sentences don't work well when read aloud. Aim for simple sentences.

3. Reflect your brand DNA

The verbal introduction sets the tone of the speaker. If you are witty, your introduction should be witty. Tom Bodett's introduction on the PBS radio show *Wait Wait ... Don't Tell Me* says this: "He writes whenever he feels like he has something to say, which is almost never." On the other hand, If you are a scholar, your intro should demonstrate that scientific fact.

4. Tune into Radio WIIFM

What's In It For Me (WIIFM) is a key radio station for your audience. Make sure your intro answers why they should put down their mobile device and listen to you.

5. Avoid complicated words

There are some words that are tough to say; try *ennui*, for example. Did you get it right? Do you see how it is one of those words that is better in writing than said aloud? If in doubt, leave it out!

6. Teach them how to pronounce your name

As I mentioned earlier, you need folks to pronounce your name correctly. Make it easy for them by having some sort of cheater device. During the 2015 Academy Awards season, for example, a TV special showcased the efforts behind the push for *The Imitation Game.* Half of the commentators referenced Harvey Wine-STINE and the other half pronounced his name Wine-STEEN. Clearly, none of us knows for sure!

WORDS OF LIZDOM

**Using Sophisticated
Words in Your Introduction—**
If you're on the fence about whether
or not a word is easy to say, follow this
mantra: if in doubt, leave it out!

In order to get the best introduction, it pays to prepare in advance. For example, I always ask who is going to introduce me. I then connect via email or phone with the introducer, review how to pronounce my name, send a current verbal introduction, and answer any questions. Of course, you'll also bring a printed verbal intro to the event (just in case they forget). It should be one page, double-spaced, and in big type so that no matter how bad the reader's eyes, your intro is an easy read.

You also have the option of selecting someone to introduce you versus merely accepting whoever the organization assigns to the task. Switching your introduction to a trusted colleague or client clearly tips the presentation in your favor: you allow for the best possible start to your talk.

See how Deanna Potter's intro sets up this petite powerhouse to succeed: "*Deanna is not your ordinary businesswoman. Instead, she is both a girly-girl with 4-inch platforms and a tomboy who knows the difference between an eyelash curler and a socket wrench. Her love of automobiles sent her on her own race where she generates winning businesses, stellar sales, and empowers others to do the same."*

Avoid clichés such as:
- Last, but not least
- First and foremost
- A speaker who needs no introduction (we all need one!)
- Without further ado

The bottom line is that you are translating your super objective of your talk into a sexy speaking title. You are then layering in a brand-appropriate verbal introduction such that you have built the expectation of exactly what the audience will get from your talk. You audience is then eager and hungry for your information, and now it's your turn to deliver! Take a hop over to the next chapter to see exactly how to create a presentation that earns rave views.

Get Gooder ... Get Going!

1. **Draft Your Bio Today**—You'll need this document for the company website, your website, your LinkedIn profile, as a credibility booster, and as a way to connect with others in the field. It's the professional tool whenever you speak.

2. **Write Your Verbal Introduction**—Remember to avoid hard-to-pronounce words or even long words; it should not take more than 60 seconds to read.

PART III
Delivering the Talk

CHAPTER 11

The Big O: How to Get Standing Ovations and Knock It Outta the Park!

Since I give over 75 talks per year, you might assume that I don't get nervous anymore. Wrong! Ask my husband: I'm a nervous wreck before any of my big events.

Virtually every presenter gets a case of the nerves. Both Katy Perry and Idina Menzel admitted to a serious case of nerves before the 2015 Super Bowl. Faced with the largest crowd in its history with 114.4 million viewers, Ms. Perry claims she grabs the nervous energy and recycles it to her advantage.

Fear of forgetting her lyrics kept singer Barbra Streisand away from live performing for over 27 years! And the founder of Bare Minerals, Leslie Blodgett, tenses up before every single QVC appearance, even though it was this channel that turned her little company into a $1.7 billion behemoth acquired by cosmetics giant Shiseido.

And often it's just like Tom Petty sings: "The waiting is the hardest part." But you can control your nerves and you can address it.

Secrets to Overcoming Nerves

1. Move Your Body

It's really hard to shake in fear when you're doing a jumping jack; trust me. If I'm behind a curtain, I'm often jumping, shaking out my hands and feet, or rolling my head. This burst of activity seems to overcome the nerves.

2. Bite Your Tongue

Really! The act of biting the tip of your tongue promotes saliva, so that you no longer feel as if your teeth are stuck to your lips.

3. Speak Positive Self-Talk

Repeat to yourself how good you are; reinforce to yourself that you are the expert; acknowledge that you've put in all of the preparation needed to deliver an outstanding talk.

4. Practice by Yourself

Even if you only have a few minutes, run to an empty room or even the restroom to test your opening out loud. Just the act of speaking your planned words starts the positive mood flowing and interrupts any negative energy.

Terry Paulson, a famed leadership speaker, also escapes to the restroom for a little practice time. He remembers once being confronted by security because he had been in there so long. The issue? It was the women's bathroom!

5. Try Vaseline

Good old-fashioned Vaseline rubbed on your lips and gums ensures that the mouth stays moist; weird, but it works!

6. Pop a Lozenge

Herbal lozenges are a speaker's best friend; try some!

7. Drink Tea

Hot tea is a great way to keep your voice smooth and your vocal cords moist.

8. Take a Big, Deep Breath

Right before I hit the stage, I've taken one huge "cleansing" breath, pushed my shoulders down, and told myself to knock it outta the park!

6 Items to Avoid Before a Speech

1. Going Out the Night Before

The current hot restaurant or bar is full of ultra-cool hard surfaces of wood, granite, concrete, and steel. In other words, all of the elements that bounce sound and cause you to scream to be heard over the cacophony. Recommendation: avoid any venue that causes you to strain your vocal cords before the big talk.

2. Carbonated Beverages

Unless you're fond of belching, I recommend saying "nyet" to the Diet Coke.

3. Dairy

Dairy products and speaking don't seem to get along very well. Milk, yogurts, and the like tend to clog up the throat, creating unwanted mucous.

4. Menthol Lozenges

Again, these interfere with your vocal cords and can cause a change in tone.

5. Antihistamine

24 hours before any talk, avoid these types of drugs. They dry up the mucous membranes, which makes it hard to swallow and speak naturally.

6. Clearing Your Throat

Clearing your throat leads to more clearing of your throat; have you ever noticed that? It's actually a physiological reaction whereby the clearing causes a mucous buildup, leading to a never-ending cycle. Nip this habit in the bud and drink water instead. If you feel a cold coming on, drink your tea, get rest, but never whisper; it strains your voice, which causes even more irritation to your voice! In a March 2015 episode of *The Good Wife*, Alicia Florrick, played by Julianna Margulies, is suffering from a cold. Her entire staff begs her to "stop talking," but the state's attorney general candidate doesn't listen. She talks on the phone throughout the show, causing her to sound like Bette Davis.

Warm Up to Succeed

Just as athletes warm up their muscles before competing, you need to warm up your voice. Vocal coach Jill Lesly Jones suggests tongue twisters, crazy limericks, and even big yawns and tongue stretches to literally get your mouth, voice, and tongue in working order. Hint: Do these exercises especially when you have an early morning speech or radio interview; it prevents you from sounding as if you just rolled out of bed!

If you can't find a favorite book of tongue twisters, here's my suggested fallback position: Dr. Seuss. Reading *Hop on Pop* or *One Fish Two Fish* is an easy way to improve your cadence and pronunciation. And you get a smile as a bonus.

Create a Pre-Speech Routine

I know, for example, that if I am traveling for a speech, I have my morning routine of warm-up exercises, speech review, and a light breakfast in my room. I don't want to mingle with anyone until I'm officially ready to go downstairs for show time. It's also another reflection of one of my rituals: I never eat before a speech. If I'm the breakfast speaker, I've had a light snack a few hours before. If I'm the luncheon speaker, I take a pass. My job is to entertain, not eat. Of course, I also believe that I need all of that energy going to my brain and not to my stomach.

Add Vocal Variety to Eliminate a B-O-R-I-N-G Speech

Variety may be the spice of life, and it certainly is the antidote to a boring talk. You must adjust pace, pause, pitch, volume, and repetition to ensure a stellar delivery. "You have the capacity to shape your voice in a way that makes people perceive you as a leader," said UCLA acoustic scientist Rosario Signorello, who conducted studies on the connection between voice qualities and audience perception.

The Power of Pacing Your Talk

Pacing is the unheralded hero of your presentation. If you are in control of your material, outline, and environment, you naturally know how to budget your time. The kiss of death is when you hear a speaker utter "We're running out of time, so let me just speed through these five slides." Wrong! The entire program deserves a set pace. Of course, you'll spend more time on key points and less time on other topics. The key is balance.

Another component of pacing is intentionally speaking faster or slower. When you're excited, go ahead and spew fast-paced info. Conversely, slow down when speaking on complicated issues.

All Pause on Deck!

Great police detectives understand pause; they intentionally let the silence hang there, knowing the accused will unconsciously try to fill that void with self-incriminating talk. You and I as speakers need to get comfortable with silence. Silence is the gong that punctuates a key point; it is the pause that lets the audience transition from one main topic to another; and it is the courageous speaker who can embrace the silence. After a particularly poignant story, pause. It's OK. Silence is often golden.

Pause is also essential to allow folks to laugh or enjoy the moment with you. You don't want to "step" on your own laugh line.

Don't Get Pitchy!

Randy Jackson of *American Idol* fame was renowned for uttering his trademark phrase of "You're a little pitchy." When it comes to speaking, this phrase refers to the tone (pitch) of your voice. Women, listen up here, as high-toned voices are known to be irritating. In fact, when a gaggle of women get together and start squealing louder, faster, and in the higher octave range, it tends to immediately cause the male audience to tune out! Generally, someone speaking in a low-pitched voice is perceived as big and dominant, while someone speaking in a high voice is perceived as small and submissive. Yikes!

A recent study from Duke University's Fuqua School of Business uncovered that male CEOs with lower-toned voices made up to $187,000 a year more than higher-pitched peers. Further, they lasted as much as five months longer as the head of a firm than their higher-pitched counterparts.

I know, you're concerned that Mother Nature gave you a high-pitched voice. I get it. Your mission as a female speaker is to speak a little lower and even a little slower. Even former Prime Minister Margaret Thatcher engaged a speech coach to bump up her volume, tone, and credibility.

Speak Louder AND Softer

If you've ever dozed off during a presentation, my guess is that monotony was the cause: an entire talk at the same volume. Varying volume not only adds interest, but signifies to your audience major sections in your talk. A loud, expansive passage signifies a big, important, wake-up moment. A soft, sotto voce moment (stage whisper) implies that you're sharing an intimate, truthful moment. By the same token, your voice naturally gets quieter when you are sharing honest, painful moments. Here's my advice: follow the natural volume of your voice, but don't be afraid to notate in your outline the moments where you especially want to get loud or soft.

Repeat for Maximum Impact

Inexperienced speakers will often let juicy nuggets of wisdom whiz by the audience's head. Wait! Slow down and repeat the lesson. That's right. Immediately after stating a key point, say it again so that the impact is felt. Remember to change it ever so slightly so that it doesn't sound like you just hit the rewind button. You don't want to repeat a point after you've spoken for a few more minutes, lest it seem that you forgot that you just told your audience that point!

Repetition also works as a good mnemonic device. Listen to the cadence of the famous Martin Luther King speech:

I have a dream that one day this nation will rise up and live out the true meaning of its creed: "We hold these truths to be self-evident: that all men are created equal."

I have a dream that one day on the red hills of Georgia the sons of former slaves and the sons of former slave owners will be able to sit down together at a table of brotherhood.

I have a dream that one day even the state of Mississippi, a desert state, sweltering with the heat of injustice and oppression, will be transformed into an oasis of freedom and justice.

This speech is often mentioned as one of the greatest speeches of all time, but it's important to note why. Of course, I've highlighted its intentional repetitive technique, but it's also a masterpiece because he avoided using notes, he adapted the talk as needed, and he wasn't afraid to broadcast his brand DNA (his church background). All of these items worked together to create the masterpiece of this talk.

WORDS OF LIZDOM

Repeat for Maximum Impact—
Don't let key lessons fly by your audience. Stop and repeat the key point, but change it just a bit for maximum impact.

Practice Makes Perfect ... Sometimes

Does it make sense to rehearse your speech? Of course! For practicing and practical purposes, try these techniques:

1. Use a Digital Recorder

When you're working solo on your speech, try talking into a digital recorder or voice app. It's the best way to gauge how you really sound. As we mentioned earlier in storytelling, it's also a good idea to listen to your story and then remove extraneous facts and commentary.

2. Practice Your Opening and Closing Stories

Remember our sandwich metaphor whereby bologna is in the middle? And our order bias, which shows that we remember the beginning and the end, but forget the middle? If this is the case, then let's nail the beginning and the end!

3. Get Comfortable with the Segues

Moving effortlessly from point to point is an underrated skill. It's the transitions that keep a speech organized and the audience on point. Try a variety of different techniques, including:

- **The Summarize-As-We-Go Approach**—"Since we've now covered how to write a bio, let's move on to the art of the verbal introduction."
- **The Additive Approach**—Pepper your talk with many organizing words, such as "next," "first," "second," "in addition to," "also," "likewise," "moreover," etc.
- **Full-Frontal Approach**—"Here's the third way to add a cool quotient to your talk." It is straightforward; what you hear is what you get!
- **Compare and Contrast**—"If a bio is for the eyes, a verbal introduction is for the ears."
- **Equal Footing**—"Just as important to a speech as the opening is the closing." Incorporate phrases such as "by the same token," "similarly," etc.
- **Sequencing**—"The first step in writing your bio is to simply bullet-point all of the key ideas. Then you can prioritize and rewrite your copy." Use these types of words to assist you

in sequencing: previously, subsequently, and then, at this time, thereafter, previously, soon, before, after, followed by, after that, next, meanwhile, formerly, finally, and during.

- **Show Me**—"As an example, Rhana Pytell changed the name of her company to Brighter Step because it showcased the positive results from her site." Use terms such as "for instance," "to illustrate," and "in this case."

4. Reality Test Your New Material

It's tough to gauge reaction when you're practicing by yourself. As speaker Mark Sanborn says: "I don't care how much you practice. You get good, ultimately, by being on the platform." So, the next time you have a new speech coming up, give a practice talk before your big talk. It's similar to Jay Leno showing up unannounced at The Comedy Store to try out his new material. He knows that there's no way to judge whether a joke will bomb or succeed except with a live audience.

Since I do high-end speaking for companies and associations, I'll agree to a gratis talk at a local chamber for the sole purpose of letting those audience members be my guinea pigs. (Shhh … they don't know that I'm trying out new material; they only know that they're getting a top-rated speaker for free.) It becomes a great win-win for both parties.

5. Practice at Different Points in Your Presentation

Have you ever heard speakers who are great at the beginning and then slowly decline as the speech goes on? Chances are that they've practiced their speech continuously from the top. I recommend to my clients that they start and pick it up from different spots. In this manner, your entire talk gets polished.

Step Away from the Lectern

Let's be clear: the lectern is the slant-topped desk that poor speakers often stand behind with a death grip; the podium is what your feet stand on to lift you up a little higher so that everyone in the room can more easily see you.

You never want to stand behind a lectern. Why?

- It blocks access to you
- It prevents natural movement and expressive gesturing
- It prevents you from moving about the room/stage
- It hinders great communication
- It creates a barrier between you and your audience

It's a sign of an inexperienced speaker—Witness General David Petraeus' mea culpa speech after his fall from grace and after resigning as CIA director. Great speakers, on the other hand, step away from the lectern and use the entire stage to engage with the audience; the closer you are physically to your peeps, the easier it is to emotionally connect as well. You can also use certain portions of the stage to signify certain emotions. As an example, I often use the right side of the stage when I tell personal stories. I then go front and center to give general guidance on improving your brand. But when it's time to share another personal story, I go right back to the right side of the stage. In essence, that space is reserved for just that emotion. It's a great technique to adopt.

The Art of Gestures

I recognize that without the lectern, it's easy to feel naked. Perhaps you're asking: what do I do with my hands? Remember to be natural, and yet when you need your hands, be definitive. No wimpy gestures allowed! Under no circumstances should you adopt a "fig leaf" pose with your hands embarrassingly over your privates. Of course, this rule also means no playing with your hair, jiggling your hands in your pockets, or doing anything else distracting. Hands are at your side, relaxed, and ready to move as naturally as possible.

Gestures are the silent communication between you and your audience. If you remember all the way back to chapter 6 where we disclosed the deadly sin of starting with a question, you'll recognize that we can ask questions to our audience later in the talk *if* we add gestures. In my video, you'll see me using all types of gestures to signify to the audience that I want to hear from them: touching my ears, using my hands, etc.

Aim to Get Rid of Your Notes

There are three ways to give a talk:

1. Via Teleprompter
2. Memorize It
3. Bulleted Memorization

Very few speakers, let alone actors, succeed via the teleprompter. It sounds just as awkward as you think it will. John Travolta became the butt of many jokes after the 2014 Oscars in which he mangled Idina Menzel's name beyond repair. Of course, the singer turned the tables on Mr. Travolta in 2015, but he still caused social media buzz for invading her privacy limits by touching her face. Or, look at Kendall Jenner at the May 2014 Billboard Awards, who admits to not being able to read well. Clearly that was the case, as she introduced the band 5 Seconds of Summer as something similar to One Direction.

If you're not using the lectern as a crutch or as a place to lean, where do you put your notes? What notes? In order to reach the pinnacle of professional speaking, you must eventually engage with your audience without PowerPoint and without notes—not an easy task.

As you master speaking, I recommend weaning yourself away from notes by first moving away from 8.5 x 11 notes to only three 3 x 5 cards with just bullet points. Then try only using one card. For every speech, set a goal of using one less index card. It's there if you need it, but try giving your talk without it. Trust me, you can do it!

WORDS OF LIZDOM

Treat Time as They Do in Vegas— Take away your watch, don't look at a clock, and make your journey with the audience timeless.

Treat Time Like They Do in Vegas!

Pretend that your talks are like Vegas—time becomes irrelevant. You take your audience on a journey, and before they know it, you've safely returned to Earth. I know one of the highest compliments I receive is when an attendee tells me that the time just flew by!

That timeless feeling can happen by coincidence or by intention. Here's how to make it work for you:

1. Never Mention Time

Don't reference it in any way whatsoever. During your Q&A, train yourself not to say, "Let me take some questions as we near the end of our time here."

2. Don't Allude to the End

No utterances of "in conclusion" or "before I wrap up."

3. Don't Mention Minutes

I'll sometimes hear a speaker announce: "For the next 45 minutes …" See how it already sounds like a jail sentence? He's already boring me in the first 2 minutes, and I've got 43 minutes yet to go!

4. Never Look at Your Watch

This is a deadly sin for a speaker, as we assume that you've timed your material so well that there's no need for you to look; you know that you are on pace.

5. Don't Use a Person as a Timer

Perhaps you've seen a person in the back of the room hold up large cards showing "5 minutes" or "3 minutes." Meeting planners believe this tactic helps keep speakers on time. In my opinion, it is utterly insulting and distracting to the speaker! Remember: you are in control of time and you don't need an elementary school tool.

WORDS OF LIZDOM

Punctuality Matters—
Great speakers start on time
and end on time. Always.

The Joy of Your Timer on Your Phone

If all of the preceding rules hint that you are aware of time without ever looking at your watch, how do you stay on schedule? You cheat!

You simply and subtly place your smartphone or iPad with the timer running on the lectern (which you won't be using) or a place where only you can see it. Turn off the ringer, but go into the "settings" feature and then into "general" options where you can regulate the "auto-lock" feature. Set it to "never" so that the phone is always on with the display. Now, as you work the room, you can easily glance down and see how much time you have left.

Start on Time and End on Time

You earn the respect of your audience and meeting organizers by always starting on time and ending on time. You'll master ending on time using the trick above, but make a promise today to start on time. If you give monthly webinars, you'll soon train your listeners to tune in a few minutes early to ensure that they'll devour every tasty morsel that you serve.

Always Prepare Bonus Material

No one ever told me this advice, so please allow me to be the first to share it: always prepare bonus material just in case....You'll need it when the preceding speaker runs short or a speaker doesn't show up or for last-minute schedule changes. Let me assure you, at some point you're going to need more material than you originally planned. When asked to step in/fill in/adjust to the change, your answer as the speaker is "No worries!" It brands you as a professional and keeps your organizers happy.

I remember being the breakfast keynote speaker in Miami, and another woman was the luncheon keynoter. She proceeded to take the stage and read, word for word, her notes for a total of 12 minutes! Since she was supposed to have spoken for 50 minutes, the frantic organizers asked me if I would return to the stage and share more material. No problema!

Bonus material also comes in handy if you happen to have slipped up and forgotten an entire section of your speech. The audience never knows, as you simply add material from your bonus session.

Have a Shortened Version of Your Speech Too

Just as you'll be asked to extend your talk, you'll undoubtedly be asked to shorten your talk. It happens all the time. Sectioning off material in your notes as "optional" allows you to easily skip over content. I laughed when an association flew me out to Columbus, Ohio, for a keynote talk planned to last 55 minutes. When I got there, they only gave me 10 minutes. Of course, I did it, and I calculated that I made $1,000 per minute for that gig!

WORDS OF LIZDOM

Always Prepare Bonus Material—
You never know when something will go awry in the program and you'll be asked to speak longer or substitute for someone; have extra content at the ready.

Get Gooder ... Get Going!

1. **Create a Pre-Speech Ritual**—Incorporate warm-ups for your mouth and body so that you're fired up to present.

2. **Schedule a Practice Arena Before Your Big Talk**—If you're worried about a big talk, schedule a practice one to truly battle-test it.

3. **Put Your Notes on 3 x 5 Cards**—Aim to get rid of notes altogether, but in the interim, put short bullets on index cards as your handy reminders. Don't forget to include when you will speak louder and when you will speak softer.

4. **Start Events on Time**—Make a pact today that all of your meetings, events, or conference calls will start and end on time.

5. **Create Bonus Material**—Commit to the practice of always having extra material you can use in an emergency.

6. **Highlight Optional Material**—Just in case your time gets cut, you'll have a fallback plan.

CHAPTER 12

Like-O-Suction: Avoiding "like" and "um" to Speak Like a Pro

Disfluency probably isn't a word you're familiar with, but I bet you've heard the utterances "um," "you know," and "so," for example. These sounds disrupt the fluency of your speech patterns. Some research suggests that they make your audience work doubly hard to comprehend the message. Worse, they lower your credibility and thereby undermine the super objective of your entire talk!

How to Identify "Speech Bumps"

I created the term "speech bumps" to refer to all of the annoying utterances that goof up a great speech. The list includes:

- And
- Like
- So
- I mean
- OMG
- Well
- Uh
- Um
- OK
- Ah
- Mmm
- Actually

- Basically
- You Know

These "filler" words occur because presenters are
1. Unaware of the problem
2. Nervous
3. Unprepared
4. Afraid of the pause
5. Speaking too fast

How to Suck Filler Words Out of Your Speech

Eliminating speech bumps is paramount. They not only waste your listeners' time, but they lower the overall impact and impression of your talk, making it difficult to get rewarded or promoted. Follow these steps to get on the smooth road of public speaking:

1. Become Aware of Your Speech Patterns

Again, your handy-dandy digital recorder is required. I can't stress enough the power of recording yourself in order to identify problems and then set a course of correction. I also suggest asking family, friends, and colleagues for help. You might also find, for example, that you toss in "throwaway" words during an interactive exercise. TV host of *Late Night* Seth Meyers recently admitted to using the phrase "That's great" even to his own embarrassment! He's now on a mission to eliminate it from his repertoire.

2. Overprepare

I'm guilty here! If you know your material forward and backward, you're less likely to fill in your presentations with fillers.

3. Get a Good Night's Rest

Verbal hiccups often occur because your mouth can't keep up with your brain! Make sure to get a good night's rest before the big presentation day.

4. Enlist Help

I was ecstatic to help *Kitchenability* author Nisa Burns eliminate "like" from her vocabulary forever. Today, you can enjoy her messages and recipes over at www.kitchenability.com

5. Create a Penalty Jar

Fabulous DJ and head of DJ MandyMixes, Mandy Rodriguez, acknowledged that she also had too many speech bumps. Her husband and daughter helped cure her at home with a fast fine of $1.00 for every inappropriate use of the word "like." Needless to say, it worked!

6. Slow Down

If you're racing against the clock or trying to squeeze too much information into too little time, your mouth won't be able to keep up!

7. Embrace the Power of the Pause

Just as we spoke about in the last chapter, a pause is powerful, but a little awkward for newbie speakers; there is a tendency to fill the blank space with filler words. Resist!

WORDS OF LIZDOM

Get Rid of Disfluencies—
To succeed, eradicate annoying speaking habits from your everyday life, and then you'll succeed in presentations too.

Assimilate Into Culture. Don't Assimilate Words!

Speakers must speak clearly. The audience must hear every word and every syllable. In fact, not understanding the lyrics seems to upset Blake Shelton on NBC's *The Voice* more than any other singing offense!

As part of your mission to speak gooder, avoid assimilation. Assimilation is simply combining two words. It's common in other languages, especially Spanish, whereby *mi hija* (my daughter) evolves into "mija." You'll notice the same process in English: the term "granma" for "grandma," for example.

Of course, there are other less acceptable assimilations which create cringe-worthy terms such as these:

> I dunno / I don't know
> Probly / Probably
> Gonna / Going to
> Wanna / Want to

My dear friend and fellow branding expert Patricia DeAngelis keeps a running list of newly created words she hears throughout the day. My fave entry? "Ammago," meaning "I am going to go." What a riot!

Upspeak: The #1 Credibility Killer in Women

Women are killing their chances of promotion, respect, rewards, and recognition with "upspeak." Upspeak (also called "valley girl speak" or "uptalk") is simply raising your voice at the end of a sentence as if it is a question when it's not.   Estimates are that when this affliction occurs, it's more likely to affect women than men. Part of the explanation is that women are conditioned for collaboration; from a very young age, women are consensus seekers, and raising our voices is informally asking for approval and buy-in.

Uptalk is often used when folks are uncertain and tentative. In fact, Thomas Linneman, a sociologist at William and Mary, recorded 100 episodes of *Jeopardy*! and analyzed 5,473 responses given during those shows. He found that both men and women used uptalk more frequently when they were giving wrong answers, showing that people use uptalk when they are feeling uncertain. But the researcher also found that a whopping 48 percent of women used uptalk even when they were answering correctly compared to 27 percent for men!

Upspeak also occurs as a result of the culture. Teenagers often want to feel a sense of belonging and therefore imitate their peers, spreading "valley girl speak" throughout the generation. Similar to fixing speech bumps, you must recognize the problem and make a commitment to combat it.

WORDS OF LIZDOM

It's Time for Like-o-Suction—
Make the commitment today to get rid of annoying words such as "like" and "um" from your presentations. Ask family and friends to keep you honest.

Learning to Love or Change Your Voice

The sound of your voice influences your brand. In a recent study by Quantified Impressions, voice quality accounted for 23 percent of listener evaluations. The content only accounted for 11 percent. Yikes!

Besides speech bumps above, there are also negative speech patterns, such as a nasal, whiny, or even a breathy tone. (Think Marilyn

Monroe singing "Happy Birthday" to JFK.) All of these traits negatively impact perception. Virtually all of them can be changed with the help of a speech therapist or coach.

If you constantly use the term "like," now is the time to rid yourself of this disease for life. Ask family and friends for help, because you must knock it out of your everyday life if you're going to succeed in not using the term during presentations.

WORDS OF LIZDOM

The Power of the Pause—
Most speech bumps occur because
the speaker is trying to fill the void with
extra words. Resist, and let a pause
simply hang with your audience.

Get Gooder ... Get Going!

1. **Identify Any Speech Bumps**—record yourself to determine if "like" or other words are invading your speech.

2. **Create a Game Plan to Fix the Fillers**—Create a penalty jar, enlist the help of family or friends, and practice knocking the fillers out of your everyday speech.

3. **Speak Your Best Even at Home**—If you're trying to get rid of poor speaking habits, start at home. Have a family member fine you for every inappropriate "like," "hmmm," or "you know." If you fix it at home, you'll bar it from the platform.

CHAPTER 13

The P's & Q's of Q&A: How to Answer Questions with Finesse

Questions aren't the usual downfall of a fabulous presentation; it's the answers! It's simply too easy as the speaker to fall down a black hole during a Q&A session. But it doesn't have to be that way. In fact, I've seen so many of my clients trip up in this area that I'm sharing how to navigate this minefield with finesse.

The Nuances of Dealing with Q&A

Here's your first rule: Never take questions at the very end of your program. I recognize that virtually all organizers think they are brilliant by reserving ten minutes for this function, but they're wrong! Taking questions at the end zaps the energy out of the room. And, as often happens, if there is only one weak question, your audience is left with the impression that there was no interest. It's not that there wasn't interest; it's that there just weren't interesting questions.

Dealing with Q&A in the Digital Age

Given our digital revolution, why not embrace the new technology? You can have audience members tweet their questions during your presentation. Simply share your Twitter handle and the hashtag. High-tech conferences will often display a rolling list of tweets so that everyone can see them at the same time.

3 Sneaky Ways to Deal with Q&A:

1. Answer Questions 75 Percent of the Way Through Your Presentation

In this way, you give great content, take questions, and then get back on track with interesting stories, examples, fun, etc., and the boring part of the question is forgotten.

2. Answer Questions After the Formal Program

Tell the audience before you conclude your program that you will stay after your program to answer questions. But don't forget to budget the time to stay.

3. Integrate Questions Throughout

I always allow my audience to ask questions throughout my talk. As I mentioned in the beginning of this book, brand-new rules demand change. And talking at your audience is simply old school. If you're embracing what I've been preaching about an engaging, interactive talk, there's simply no need for a separate Q&A session, as you've been answering questions throughout your presentation!

In order for spontaneous questions to take place, you must foster that environment by letting your audience know that their input is welcome. You can make a joke as I often do, telling my audience that I already have a 17-year-old who doesn't talk to me, so I invite them to please talk to me! You can use your hand gestures to make it clear that you want to hear from them. And you can boldly ask, "Did I hear a question there?" It's also a good idea to ask for questions before moving on to the next section or main points.

WORDS OF LIZDOM

Dealing with Q&A—
Never answer questions at the end of
your talk. It zaps the energy out of the room
and ends the speech on a low note.

Answering Questions Takes Practice

Newbie speakers often fall into a gaping hole when taking questions, because no one ever practices this skill! Here's a suggestion: deliver your talk to a dear friend, colleague, or family member, and let them fire away with questions. Here are a few rules to make you a success while answering questions:

Repeat the Question

This tactic isn't stalling; it's instilling understanding for your audience. Most of the time, a question from the audience isn't understood correctly. By repeating it, you clarify the question and allow everyone to appreciate the answer. In our YouTube world, repeating the question also allows for the question to be heard on the video or audio recording of your talk.

Never Remark "Great Question"

Ugh! I hate to hear this type of response, as it just reeks of stalling and kissing up. Also avoid "Glad you asked" and other faux compliments. Just answer the question matter-of-factly and move on!

You Are Not Obligated to Provide All the Answers

Yep, I really wrote that. It is *not* your responsibility to find out all of the answers to questions that might be asked at your talk. Often they are beyond the scope of the talk, they are relevant only to that individual, or they require proprietary research. Repeat after me: I don't have to have all the answers. (Feel better now?)

Keep Your Answers Short

Many individuals ask questions to make themselves look good and to grab the limelight; keeping your answers short keeps the momentum going.

It May Be Out of the Scope

I often get asked if I can create a tagline for an audience member. I laugh it off, but say something like, "Of course, I can help, and I charge for that service. Please see me afterward so I can finalize the contractual details with you."

Encourage Someone Else to Find Out the Answer

If the question is relevant to the group, but still requires a ton of work, ask for a volunteer who might want to do the research and report back.

Invite the Asker to See You Privately

If the question is complicated, don't think twice about inviting them to see you afterward. It's a great compromise solution.

Answer Questions with Respect

This is not the time to say, "As I mentioned …" This phrase insults the audience member who obviously didn't hear or understand you. Simply answer in a straightforward manner.

Never Lose Control of the Room

Regardless of the atmosphere, don't lose control. Make sure you remain in charge.

Questions can be a slippery slope, but especially as a newer speaker, you'll want to pay close attention to the type of questions your audience is asking.

WORDS OF LIZDOM

You Don't Have to Have All the Answers—
It's OK to not know the answer to all of the questions. In fact, you can also delegate the answer to someone else in the room if the question is of interest to only a narrow target.

Get Gooder ... Get Going!

1. **Practice Answering Questions with a Colleague**—Grab a friend and a glass of wine! Seriously, you must make time to practice answering questions, and this is a case where practicing on your own won't help.

2. **Get Comfortable Delegating an Answer**—Listen carefully to the type of questions coming up again and again in your talks. They could signify areas that need more time, explanation, or examples.

3. **Tune in to the Questions Asked**—Listen carefully to the type of questions coming up again and again in your talks. They could signify areas that need more time, explanation, or examples.

4. **Create Your Own FAQs for Practice**—Brainstorm all of the potential questions that an audience member can ask; get clear answers on those so you're ready for them.

CHAPTER 14

Remember the "F" Word—FOLLOW-UP!

Some marketing experts claim that it's all about "showing up," but I believe in the power of following up. It is the follow-up that gets you rewarded, promoted, and presented with amazing opportunities. In fact, I use follow-up tests to determine if I'll hire an employee, engage an intern, or work with a vendor. I'm testing them to ensure that they understand the power of attending to the final details.

Creating Systems That Work

You therefore need a system for attending to all of the nitty-gritty details that fall into the follow-up category. One of my favorite techniques is to use a small notebook and write ALL of the promises I made. For example, you may get a question from your CEO that demands an answer. Instead of simply committing to getting back to her, write it down and get buy-in for when it's really due.

By the same token, you'll also get individual questions and requests from attendees. I've found that writing a note on the back of their biz card rarely works because typically (and I do the same thing), the card gets thrown away after you've scanned the contact information. Again, put the request in the notebook.

The more follow-up you get after a talk, the more opportunities to re-engage with your audience. In other words, stop looking at the "F" word as an inconvenience but as a treasure trove of opportunity. If, for example, during Q&A, your attendees really want your 15 techniques for closing the sale, you now have a solid, meaty reason for sending them an email.

WORDS OF LIZDOM

Embrace the "F" Word—
The greater the follow-up after
the talk, the greater the opportunity to
re-engage with your audience.

The Power of Email Follow-Up

Despite the explosive growth in social media, email marketing continues to outperform other communication vehicles in terms of turning prospects into clients. And if you've just given a presentation, your brand is top of mind with the audience, allowing you to strengthen the relationship. I've found that the best way to stay engaged with your audience is through a content-rich follow-up email. Remember: content is king with a follow-up campaign. More than 80 percent of the time you are purely giving value; only 20 percent of your email is promotional.

Remaining top of mind means that you don't simply send one follow-up email, but create an entire campaign of valuable information, determining the length and frequency of your missives. I send, for example, a specific email after each talk, and then share my blog with them weekly. My Words of Lizdom blog has been in existence for over 16 consecutive years, and most folks remain on my list for an average of 11 years! You can sign up at www.redfirebranding.com.

In 2000 I did a speech for media companies hosted by Nielsen, the marketing research company that measures TV viewership. However, I wasn't hired by one of the attendees, Univision, until 2008. The executive in charge stated that she never forgot me because of my weekly emails.

In order to have the shortest lag time between giving a speech and sending a follow-up email to your audience, I recommend that you write the email in advance. Really! You can always tweak it based upon the questions you received at the event, but it's faster to edit an email than to start from scratch.

Stop Your Fear of Phoning

Virtually everyone today is both enamored and comfortable with email. But it's not the only communication tool available. Your notebook questions might require a meaty answer or substantive conversation. If so, pick up the phone!

Linking in with Social Media

LinkedIn is, of course, the business tool of choice. You can employ a system of not only following up via email with all of your attendees, but connecting with them on this platform too. Don't forget other social media too. It's easy to find and follow folks on Twitter, and you can tweet your answer directly to attendees if they have a Twitter account.

The Goodgolden Rules of Raffles

I've found that the best way to stay connected and create that strong bond with your attendees is through email. But if you just announce at the front of the room that you'd like to market to everyone there, you'll probably be met with deaf ears. So your secret weapon is creating a fun raffle with a prize that your attendees actually want to win. In order to turn your raffle at your speaking event into a red-hot success, just follow these rules:

1. Never Raffle Off Your Own Stuff

The minute you offer your own book, session, or CD, is the moment your sales go down. Why? Everyone in the room believes they'll be the lucky winner and therefore they have no need to purchase it from you.

2. Ensure the Raffle Bowl Is Brand-Appropriate

A generic raffle bowl is the antithesis of branding, so create a raffle receptacle that is relevant to your brand in terms of color or theme.

3. Select and Pack an Easily Portable Raffle Bowl

I've seen fabulous large martini glasses, but I know glass and traveling don't work well together. Instead, look for lightweight options that travel easily. You can never rely on the venue to offer up a bowl that will work.

4. Ask Your Helper to Collect Cards

Passive collecting of business cards won't grow your email list or your influence. Instead, weave in to your talk the raffle prize, and then have your helper go around to collect the business cards. Your goal is to collect the contact information of 90 percent of those in attendance.

5. Select a Great Raffle Prize

No one wants a free insurance audit, so select a prize that people actually covet. Starbucks cards, for example, have become so ubiquitous that they have lost perceived value. Storyteller Karen Dietz hit a home run by teaming up with Storyteller Wines for her raffle prize.

6. Don't Buy the Prize

In this world of joint ventures, you don't need to buy the raffle gift. Typically you can get it donated, because you'll feature the winning brand in the talks, at your table, or even on your website. Former client Benita Davis Webber, creator of Ripple Textile Recycling, has The Container Store donate gift cards to her Parent-Teacher Association (PTA) events.

7. Create Raffle Slips

Although business cards are the preferred currency, approximately 20 percent of your audience at an event won't have them. Allow everyone to participate by creating and having on hand a raffle slip to use in place of the biz card.

Try Self-Evaluations

If you are a new speaker or on a mission to become a phenomenal speaker, start employing speaker evaluations now! Distribute an evaluation form so that your attendees can write what they might be afraid to say. Of course, then offer up an option to remain anonymous. I arm my clients with speaker evaluations so that they start on a path of continual improvement, but you can follow these rules to create your own document:

1. Only Ask a Few Questions

You can only ask about five questions after an event. Remember: It is a quick survey, not a full-blown questionnaire.

2. Balance Quant and Qual Questions

Qualitative questions allow the writers to answer the questions however they see fit. It often then makes sense to include a few qualitative questions in your evaluations. You'll also get longer comments and even comments that would work as a testimonial (for example, "You were fabulous!"), but you won't be able to make diagnostic conclusions (for example, 90 percent of the room rated the presentation a "5" on a 5-point scale). On the other hand, quantitative questions must be answered on a scale of 1–5 or in a close-ended manner to allow you to reach scientific conclusions Example: How valuable was today's talk in terms of helping you with your career?

a. Extremely valuable
b. Very valuable
c. Somewhat valuable
d. Not valuable at all
e. Worthless

3. Read the Comments, but Try to Remain Unaffected

Yep, it hurts to read negative reviews, but if the comments are specific, you can use them to improve. You might uncover "speech bumps" that no one dared tell you before, awkward segues between topics, or even confusing concepts that weren't presented clearly. Look at them, create a plan, and then throw them away! Every single speaker has bombed, and dwelling on your mistakes won't help.

WORDS OF LIZDOM

Follow-Up Email—
Write the email for every speech before your event; in this manner, you have the shortest lag time between delivery and follow-up.

Don't forget that the art of giving a speech is not only providing valuable information but also starting a conversation with your audience members. Look for ways to engage, remain connected, and even work together. And the secret to all of these opportunities is follow-up!

Get Gooder ... Get Going!

1. **Decide Upon Your Raffle Bowl**—Consider height, color, weight, and brand DNA.

2. **Determine Who You Can Partner with for Prizes**—I hate to see entrepreneurs pay for their raffle prizes. Instead, start thinking of who else might want to reach your target audience.

3. **Create a Self-evaluation Form**—Keep it short and easy for your audience.

PART IV
Insider Secrets as a Paid Speaker, Employee, or Entrepreneur

CHAPTER 15

Bon Voyage: Launching Your PAID Speaking Career

If you've moved from being a good speaker to a great speaker, it might also be time for you to transition to becoming a phenomenal professional speaker. Remember, however, that the basic goals of speaking don't change; just the scale, scope, and pay.

Listen to Yourself

An essential ingredient en route to improving your speaking delivery is to listen to yourself. I recommend recording every single speech you give on a digital recorder and then listening to the recording. Yes, it can be painful to listen to yourself, but it's the only way to recognize your speech bumps, pausing, pacing, or volume issues. Take notes and see if you liked yourself. Were you entertained?

Now video your talks. I recommend video *after* audio so that you get comfortable with your own voice before fretting about your appearance. Virtually every woman I coach comments about her hair (me too!), but you are now seeing what your audience sees. Now, look at how you command the stage, your gestures, and your connection and interaction with the audience. Take notes for improvement.

Call in a Professional

Even armed with your notes, it's virtually impossible to improve without professional help. You may see what's not working but still not be able to fix it. Consider hiring a coach who can add unparalleled value.

I worked with Tammy Rimes, for example, who is a fiery redhead just like me. She often spoke at government conferences for an employer, but her goal was to quit her day job and get paid to speak about topics that excited her. From sales to teamwork to living the dream life, Tammy finished 2014 with ten paid speeches!

Sometimes you need to improve your speaking ability at the office. I work with many employees and executives who know they need a little help in hitting a home run of a presentation. Monica Kling, who works at NRG, wanted to ensure that her recommendations were accepted in a speech to her CEO. In just two short hours, we reorganized her talk and even added an interactive component so that her executive team didn't sleep through her talk! She nailed her talk and was asked to present at a national sales team meeting.

WORDS OF LIZDOM

**Embrace a Path of
Continuous Improvement—**
Never stop improving. Even with years of
experience, seek feedback, experts, coaches, and mentors
for improving your speaking performance.

How to Get Speaking Gigs

The number-one issue all speakers struggle with is how to get more speeches. Here's how to start getting gigs:

1. Start Building a Niche

I trust that there are a few fields in which you've worked extensively. I've delivered many speeches for the disc jockey association, which has a very heavy reliance upon weddings. I then leveraged that experience to speak for The Special Event (the huge industry annual convention), WIPA (Wedding Industry Professionals Association), the International Caterers Association, and tons of other wedding-related associations.

2. Determine Trade Associations for This Niche

The person who coordinates speeches can have titles such as

- Director of Training
- Director of Meetings and Conferences
- Head of Development
- Conference Coordinator
- VP of Meetings
- Meeting Planner

3. Call the Meeting Planner AFTER Reviewing the Website

Call and make a pitch and be ready to follow up immediately with your speaker packet.

4. Identify Companies in Your Niche

Sometimes it's easier to get hired as the trainer than as a keynoter. You might be able to get your foot in the door through "lunch and learn" type programs. There typically is already a formula, schedule, and a small honorarium available. You can always parlay a short talk into a bigger gig.

5. Ask Clients and Contacts for Referrals

It's always easy to make a warm phone call to a prospect than a cold call. Create a "hit list" of the top ten companies and associations that you've targeted and keep asking until you find someone who knows someone. Then you can make your first call.

6. Connect with Other Speakers

At first blush, it seems foolish to say that other speakers are a good source of business, but it's true. If a colleague was a keynoter for the big convention last year, it's rare for him to be the returning speaker this year. But he can refer you to the event, and you can do the same for him. Become a member of the National Speakers Association (www.nsaspeaker.org) to connect with other speakers.

7. Start Speaking ASAP

Speaking is your best advertising! I often use my 20/20 rule in speaking for free: 20 minutes and within 20 miles of my home. In order to profit from these talks, you must make it clear that you're actively looking for other talks, and even distribute a combination evaluation form (adding to your mission of constantly improving) and leads form. Boldly ask what other groups would benefit from a talk from you. You can either follow up or have your sales professional make these follow-up calls.

The Truth About Bureaus and Agencies

Wannabe speakers dream of having their phone ringing endlessly with calls and gigs from speaking bureaus, but that is hardly the reality. As you'll see below, I'm not the biggest fan of either agencies or bureaus, because they take a big bite out of your speaking fee. Most speakers use a variety of these techniques:

Speaker Bureaus

These are agencies that work with clients (meaning companies or associations) that are putting on a conference. Truthfully, these types of businesses wield less power than ever before, as clients can find speakers on their own with a simple visit to Google. Also remember that as a speaker, you are NOT the client; you are the chattel who fills a need, as I've been reminded by many agencies. The bureau gets paid its commission—usually 20 to 30 percent of your fee—regardless of who speaks! As a result, you'll find bureaus are rarely interested in cultivating a relationship, finding out about you, or promoting you over another speaker. Of course, then, bureaus do not require any type of exclusive contract with you.

Speaker Agencies

These are agencies that become your exclusive representation. They field all queries about you, create your contracts, confirm your calendar bookings, etc. Even if you book a speech on your own, the agency takes its commission. Again, most agencies do not make outbound calls on your behalf, but rather wait for your phone to ring.

Sales Professionals

Most speakers today employ someone who "dials for dollars." This technique is most efficient and effective, as they are working for you or only a few other noncompetitive speakers. They understand you as a speaker, your programs, and your strengths. Their commission is typically smaller than a bureau (15%) and they have a great deal of success. If you are a newbie speaker, you'll be making these calls yourself, and that's okay; usually the best salesperson for you is YOU!

The Difference Between a Free Speech and a Rainmaker Speech

As you just read, I will often take an unpaid speech if it's within 20 miles, but it must also be a good fit. And therein lies the difference between a rainmaker speech and a free speech. A free speech is pure practice for you; it's not necessarily the perfect audience. A rainmaker speech is peppered with prospects that are so valuable to you that you would pay them! A perfect example of a rainmaker speech for me is San Diego Women's Week; it's packed with female entrepreneurs and executives who are often looking to hire brand consultants and coaches.

Negotiating for Items Besides Money

Your nemesis as a speaker will soon become the refrain, "But we don't pay for speakers." As a newly minted speaker, there are tons of items that you want and need that you can negotiate for in place of a fee. In fact, I've created a handout for clients entitled *99 Items to Negotiate When They Can't Pay Your Fee.*

WORDS OF LIZDOM

Become Friends with Your Fellow Speakers—
Developing friendships with speakers gives you an opportunity to learn from others, bounce ideas off them, reality-check shifts in the market or new players, and even get referrals.

As you work with the meeting organizers, you must recognize that everything besides money is usually negotiable. Ask about room upgrades, limo transportation, spa treatments, companion airfare, or even video of your presentation in lieu of your regular fee.

Be Wary of Scam Artists

Remain on high alert for companies preying on new speakers. Be wary of bureaus asking you to pay a fee to appear on their website or to appear in a showcase. A "showcase" is typically a full-day event with a nonstop parade of speakers who are "auditioning" in front of meeting planners. In reality, these events are poorly attended by meeting planners, and in some cases the only folks in the audience are the speakers waiting to go on next! These faux events make a ton of money for the organizer, who charges speakers for the privilege of speaking. Wrong!

Just last week, a small cadre of San Diego-based speakers shared information about a ruthless man who continues to ask you to put "hold" dates on your calendar for a speaking event that will never appear. He then turns around and asks you for a deposit! And here's an even more egregious example: one of my clients flew all the way over to Thailand for a speech, only for the bureau to go bankrupt and leave her with unpaid expenses. The lesson: never travel outside of your state without all of your expenses covered.

At least once a year I'm invited via email to give a speech in Asia. The conference at first blush looks interesting, but then the invitational email includes this text: "Covered expenses include coach airfare from San Diego to Kuala Lumpur." Ugh! Not only does this frugality cause me alarm, but once I google the organization, I find blatant reports of the group not paying its speakers. In other words, speakers are vocal, and the Internet allows everyone to post complaints via social media. If a company, especially a foreign one, has a bad reputation, you'll likely read about it. Please perform your "duh diligence" or "due diligence" by connecting with other speakers and researching clients.

Look for Piggyback Opportunities

Once you're traveling for a speech, doing an incremental speech doesn't take significantly more time or effort. After all, travel just ain't glamorous anymore! So if you're traveling to Baltimore, for example, explore speaking opportunities in Washington, D.C., Annapolis, or even Alexandria, Virginia. You're able to offer your speaking services for a screaming deal and without travel fees.

Speaker Antarctic Mike Pierce is brilliant about leveraging his travel schedule. He religiously uses LinkedIn and his database to connect with others when visiting a new city.

WORDS OF LIZDOM

Diversify Your Revenue Sources—
Even as a paid professional speaker,
ensure that you derive other revenue from
products, coaching, or consulting to ensure
that you can survive any downturns
in the economy.

The One-Sheet:
The ONLY Marketing Piece You Need

The good news is that the digital world has changed everything when it comes to the speaking business. In the "old" days of 2000, you needed printed one-sheets, a VHS demo reel, custom folders, and printed photographs that made up your amazing speaking packet. Yikes!

Today you print virtually nothing, but you do need a one-sheet. But you're probably asking, "What is a one-sheet and why do I need one?" The term might be a tad antiquated, because now virtually all speakers create an electronic PDF that is actually two pages, but it acts as the Cliff's Notes of your career: a short summary of who you are and why a meeting planner should hire you.

Prepare your one-sheet item *before* you contact any association, bureau, agent, or meeting planner, because you will undoubtedly be asked for it before your phone conversation is finished. It's considered the lifeblood of their business, and if it takes one to three months from the time you whet a prospect's interest until the time you send them your one-sheet, their taste for booking you may have soured.

WORDS OF LIZDOM

**Create a Low-Resolution
One-Sheet for Easy Emailing—**
Have your graphic designer specifically create
a low-resolution one-sheet PDF that is faster and smaller
to email than the high-resolution one on your site.
Your recipients will thank you for not
clogging up their inbox.

Four Benefits of a One-Sheet

1. Establishes credibility—Not just by the information provided, but also by virtue of you even having one!
2. Summarizes you, your career, and the benefits to your audience.
3. Explains why you are different from other speakers.
4. Details the specific programs that you offer.

Essential Components of a One-Sheet

One-sheets vary dramatically from person to person, but your one-sheet *must* contain:

1. Your Brand DNA
2. Photo
3. Brief Bio
4. Benefits/Outcomes of Listening to You
5. Speech/Workshop Titles
6. Testimonials/Client List
7. Call to Action
8. Contact Info

The speaking business is a crazy and competitive one! It can be profitable, but it takes a ton of effort to make the work look effortless. Making the transition to a paid speaking career means treating it like a business. Set up a separate business account, get good at negotiating and selling, utilize contracts, and have fun!

WORDS OF LIZDOM

Revenues Before Expenses—
As a new speaker, you'll need many items, but prioritize your spending list and focus on revenue before expenses.

Get Gooder ... Get Going!

1. **Start Recording Your Talks Today**—Now is the time to start on your continual path of improvement. Listen to yourself and take notes on what you want to improve.

2. **Introduce Yourself as a Speaker**—If folks don't know you're a speaker for hire, it's hard to get hired as a speaker. And make sure "speaker" is on your business card too!

3. **Create Your One-Sheet**—Start putting all of your elements together and then hire a graphic designer; the do-it-yourself look won't work here.

CHAPTER 16

Perks, Promotions, and Praise:
How to Speak Gooder On the Job

We all know the drill: huddle into a room, turn down the lights, and project your slides on the screen. B-O-R-I-N-G! PowerPoint is an informational tool; great for sharing facts and figures, but easily used incorrectly. Either too much information on a slide ("You probably can't read this, but ...") or not enough to make the point. PowerPoint has become so ubiquitous that it's spawned a satirical game entitled PowerPoint Karaoke. Office workers are presented with a deck of slides that they have never seen before, and they must then ad-lib commentary! Search YouTube for samples.

Eight Sneaky Ways to Avoid
Death by PowerPoint

1. Visuals Rule

If you must use slides, think of Al Gore's presentation of "An Inconvenient Truth." It was a steady stream of high-impact visuals, images, and videos that popped. Stop using text if one high-quality image will suffice.

2. Don't Read Your Slides

No leader today advances through the ranks by regurgitating what's on screen. You must summarize and highlight for the audience.

3. Key In to Key Data

If you're showing a chart or graph, showcase a certain blip; point out the reason for us.

4. Write Sexy Headlines vs. Titles

Here's another good use for the information we learned in chapter 9. Create compelling, interesting headlines instead of boring labels. Compare "Problems with Younger Generation and Reaching Target" to "Top 2 Reasons Teens Don't Like Us."

5. Use a Large Font

No one ever complains about your slides being too easy to read.

6. Less Is More

Don't overwhelm or overcrowd your slides with excessive data; it's more important to present the information than worry about how many slides you're using.

7. Never Turn Your Back

Can you see how insulting it is to turn your back on your audience? It literally and figuratively feels insulting. If you are turning around to see your own slides, it's time to create better notes or a PC with your own slides in front of you to prevent this move.

WORDS OF LIZDOM

Never Turn Your Back on an Audience—
If you're turning around to look at your own slides, you are insulting your audience twofold: 1) by not looking them in the eyes, and 2) by demonstrating that you haven't prepared your material well enough to know what's next.

8. Add an All-Black Slide

Swedish speaker Johan Ronnestam recommends shaking up your colleagues with one solid black slide. It forces you to deliver then and there your key point that will have them spellbound.

Can You Kick PowerPoint to the Curb?

Most importantly, determine if you even need a slide presentation. Could you distribute an outline, agenda, or even a fill-in-the-blank handout? A free sample of a fill-in-the-blank handout is available when you register your book at www.speakgooder.com/bonus. These items might be a refreshing substitute for your PowerPoint.

Rehearse More Than You Think You Need To

I'll admit it: rehearsing is boring! You feel that way, I feel that way, and your competitors at work feel that way. So how do you get a leg up on them? You rehearse longer and stronger. You might even get a coach. But the ultimate goal is for you to wow your supervisors each and every time. You will quickly earn a reputation as an amazing speaker. And amazing speakers are the ones who get promoted, get invited to bigger stages, and get offered the opportunities of a lifetime.

Keep a Quip on Your Hip

Many workers feel scared to present to colleagues or superiors who they view as known strangers; they're familiar, but they don't know a lot about them. One way to start turning colleagues into companions is to learn a little more about them. In fact, here's an easy way for you to start the ball rolling: keep a quip on your hip. It's simply an interesting fact or tidbit that you can easily throw into a conversation or trot out in response to the standard question of "What's new?" The goal of a quip is to start a dialogue so that you eventually have something to discuss with somebody to start building rapport.

I like to create quips that demonstrate your credibility or expertise. For example, one of my clients is a marketing researcher. She is also on a mission to discover the best hamburger in Los Angeles, so she keeps a killer spreadsheet evaluated by ten key criteria. She invites all of the people from her interactions to complete a questionnaire, and then shares the responses to date. The survey is a hoot while also demonstrating that her core competency is research.

Create a New Normal

Having spent a few years at Quaker Oats, I'm used to the refrain of "But we don't do it that way here." If you're trying to get noticed and get ahead, you might have to try something different. If, for example, the recommended formula for presenting to the CEO is a 15-minute monologue, you might have to break the rules and insert a short video. Or present with your colleagues. Or create a discussion. Or ditch the typical template. Nothing creates a headwhip faster than seeing something different. You are looking for new and interesting ways to conquer the same old thing.

Another way to brand out and stand out is to slowly start your revolution without saying a word. The idea of starting a meeting late and waiting for everyone to show up is anathema to me. If you feel the same way, you can simply start your meetings promptly, and folks will adapt to your new normal.

When I was acting vice president at NEXT Proteins, I utilized a bit of R&D (Rip off and Duplicate) from Quaker Oats and had my team start every weekly meeting with a 5-minute competitive presentation. Each member had to present a product, its positioning, promotion, pricing, and serve it up. Tasting the product along with hearing about it made the presentations interesting and sometimes delicious!

Let Interactivity Enter the Room

Every talk deserves interaction. It could be as simple as designating a time to discuss what you have proposed or letting your room digest the new information. For one client who was making the argument for getting a vanity toll-free phone number (example: 800-I-FLY-SWA or 800-GO-FEDEX), we had everyone pull out their phone and dial customer service. Not one single employee could remember the number! Voilà! Her proposal was approved.

Become the Star

Your presentation isn't about the slides or the room; it's about you. Use your tech toys as backup, but make sure you walk in as if you own the room. Make everyone comfortable; adjust the room temperature if necessary. Implement a brave change of bringing coffee or refreshments. Use strong gestures, walk purposefully, and keep eye contact. It's all about you setting up you for success!

WORDS OF LIZDOM

Create a New Normal—
Stop waiting for your organization to change and try changing it yourself. Introduce a new template, a new formula, and a new agenda.

Get Gooder ... Get Going!

1. **Determine How You Could Change the World at Your Office**—Can you introduce a new template? Can you get rid of PowerPoint?

2. **Introduce Interactivity to Every Meeting**—It could be as simple as having partners discuss an agenda item for two minutes or creating a ten-minute group discussion.

3. **Over-Rehearse Your Presentation**—It's worth it!

CHAPTER 17

Showing Off! Speaking to Sell Your Services and Close the Sale

Out of 18 client-getting activities, guess which is the fastest way to convert prospects into clients? Speaking! If engineered correctly, speaking demonstrates your knowledge and expertise to such an extent that audiences are literally begging for you to work with them. However, many newbie entrepreneurs make these critical mistakes:

Overdelivering a Promotional Message

A speech is not a selling opportunity, but a telling opportunity. You don't need to tell your audience the benefits of working with you when you can demonstrate the success of your clients instead. The implication is clear that you were the one who engineered the result.

Taking the Credit

Allow your staff or clients to revel in the praise, not you. If your audience hears about the positive return on investment from a project that you've engineered, they'll know it was you; you don't need to remind them.

Explaining the Why and Not the How

This formula of never telling your audience how to do anything is the fastest way to alienate your audience. Yes, it's recommended by many advocates of the "speak to sell" school of thought, but I abhor it! If your audience has spent its time and money to hear you speak, they deserve to walk away with quality content. Of course, you couldn't possibly share all of your secrets during a keynote, but you had better share some of them!

Fear of Giving It All Away

Many entrepreneurs and even authors fret that if they talk about how they do something, there'll be no need to hire them. Wrong! Similar to the old Syms slogan, "An educated consumer is our best customer," the more your prospects understand the difficulty of the process, the more likely they are to recognize that it's simpler to just hire you. For example, I could speak for four hours about how to create a winning brand name, but that doesn't mean that you'll be able to name anything easily by yourself. The hurdles are simply too great in combining creativity with domains and trademark issues.

Pick the Right Audience

If you are using speaking as a business-building tool, it only pays dividends if you are speaking in front of the right audiences. Chamber events, for instance, might be a fabulous audience in Silicon Valley, but if your local chamber is composed of solopreneurs and you're trying to sell the "C" suite (CEOs or CFOs), you'll need a different platform. Don't forget about Vistage, which has many C-suite groups only.

As you negotiate your talk, even if you are giving it for free, please make sure that your audience has to pay something. If they pay nothing, they think it's worth nothing. For a talk I gave to Petco's best corporate customers, we asked for a donation to The Humane Society to secure their reservation vs. a paid fee; it was a win-win because the charitable organization was relevant to Petco's brand, and it ensured that the audience had a little skin in the game.

Hosting Your Own Event or Seminar

A viable alternative to finding an organization to host you is to create your own event. Of course, this route requires getting a venue, providing a reception table, handling reservations, getting food secured, and having a robust email list to literally get butts in seats. Most seminar speakers will tell you that this last element is the toughest: getting attendees. You will have to email many invitations, send confirming emails, and follow up to make it work; but once you have the system in place, it makes it easy to repeat. I am a fan of the automated system of Infusionsoft; it's a robust email, customer relationship management software system, back-end sales, and an amazing tool for speakers. Take a demo drive and you'll see for yourself.

And if you are hosting your own event, without a small price for admission, you can't rely on the head count and get the right amount of seats, food, or parking. Trust me: free seminars in the business-to-business world do not work.

WORDS OF LIZDOM

Spill the Beans to Lure Clients—
Give up on the old-school formula
of sharing the WHY and not the HOW at
your speeches. Your audience deserves to walk
away with a few tangible and useful ideas that
demonstrate your expert status.

Picking the Right Format

If you are sharing specific, targeted information, a 20-minute format might not be able to tackle a meaty topic. Instead, a longer "lunch and learn" or two-hour workshop might be a better option. And the longer you speak, the higher your credibility, and the higher your opportunity to sell a high-ticket item. To put it in plain English, it's virtually impossible to sell a $10,000 benefit plan after speaking for less than 30 minutes. But within a four-hour talk, closing the sale is within reason.

Sell the Brand YOU!

Since the primary purpose that you are speaking is to sell, astute entrepreneurs recognize that their audience is figuratively "buying" them. As a result, you want to share a little more about you and your life. Of course, your audience wants to hear about your clients' success, but they are also looking for a glimpse into you and how you work. Are you a morning person? Do you have kids? Do you have high ethics? Are you a rabid consumer of popular culture? All of these answers influence the decision to hire you.

In 2015, news anchor Deborah Norville said that the reason for her longevity on TV is that her audience knows her so well. She believes her audience knows that she has three kids, but also that she delivers a news segment with integrity and without the will to "screw somebody."

Keep Track of Your Metrics

In order to continually pick the right audience, it helps to measure your results. I encourage all of my clients to measure:
- The total percentage of the room that purchased from you
- The percentage of men vs. women who purchased
- The percentage of self-employed vs. employees who purchased
- The percentage who purchased in different age groups
- The average purchase price of what was sold

If you sell a product in the back of the room and track your metrics, for example, you'll know quickly enough that you closed 33% of the room; 90% of your buyers were women; the percentage of entrepreneurs vs. employees who purchased was 50%, and the average purchase price was $497. You can then forecast your return on investment for future events and match your demographics accordingly. It also arms you with the knowledge to accept or reject gigs.

I know, for example, that men virtually never buy from me after a talk. My reasoning? Because they don't want to admit that they don't have all of the answers. They will purchase and invest in me, but it's always after the event when they can buy without the scrutiny of their colleagues around them.

WORDS OF LIZDOM

Pick the Right Audience and Venue—
If they pay nothing, it's worth nothing. If the audience hasn't paid anything to attend the seminar, it's doubtful they'll invest in you either.

Get Gooder ... Get Going!

1. **Investigate Appropriate Groups and Formats for Delivering Your Talks**—Find out about the typical cost to attend and the audience demographics. Don't be afraid to suggest an innovative format that best fits you and your targets' needs.

2. **Track Your Metrics**—Are you more successful with women vs. men? Which audiences schedule follow-up appointments with you? How do you get more of those types of people?

Index of Names

Acknowledgments

This book has been in the making for almost 19 years! It is built upon every misfire, mistake, and misstep that I have made in pursuit of speaking gooder. Most importantly, it's a grand culmination of all my work with great corporations, trade associations, employees, executives, and entrepreneurs who have put their trust in me.

My tribe of coaching clients keeps me on my toes; they know that I have the courage to tell them that "their baby is ugly," and yet they know how to turn the tables and tell me the same. They voted on this cover, argued with me over the final content, and allowed me to use their name and stories. Thank you!

Bethany Kelly and I fortuitously met over a Thanksgiving dinner, and for her guidance, pushing, pressing, and persevering, I am most grateful. To Lisa Schulteis, my Infusionsoft expert and web guru who keeps my technology working, I'm honored to call you my friend.

In order to devote time to this project, I camped out at Hera Hub in San Diego, a coworking space for female entrepreneurs. For the great support, feedback, and copious cups of coffee, I am grateful.

To my son with his wicked sense of humor, I'm proud to be your mom. And to my current and last husband Patrick, you ease my monkey mind, provide endless fodder for tweets that cannot be tweeted, and make my life sweeter.

Of course, any errors are still mine, and you can tell me all about them with a simple email to Liz@redfirebranding.com.

Liz Goodgold

About the Author

How to Brand Out, Stand Out, and Cash In on Your Biz!

Liz is an author, coach, consultant, and motivational "speecher" who shares how to brand out, stand out, and cash in on your business. In fact, her clients typically boost their income by at least 40 percent after working with her!

Big Company, Big Stage Experience

This fiery redhead has engaged audiences at Pfizer, Warner Brothers, Abbott Labs, Qualcomm, and over 150 other companies and associations. She is a former brand manager at Quaker Oats, business editor at Times Mirror, and lowly book "schlepper" at Macmillan Publishing. She gives over 75 talks per year across the globe, including Hawaii, Canada, and China.

Media Maven Dishing the Dirt on Branding

Liz has appeared on virtually every news station, including CNN, CNBC, NBC, ABC, CBS, PBS, and perhaps even PMS. Her quick wit and quips get her quoted in *The Huffington Post*, *The New York Times*, *Fortune*, and *The Wall St. Journal*. She was the branding columnist for *Entrepreneur* magazine, reaching over 1.1 million readers per month. You can hear her sexy sound bites as the celebrity branding expert on *Hollywood Scandals* for seasons 1 and 2.

Biz Author Who Serves Up Business-Boosting Strategies

Based upon her consulting and coaching, Liz shares strategies that work in all three of her books: *How to Speak Gooder*, *Red Fire Branding*, and *DUH! Marketing*. Liz recognizes the value of R&D: *Ripping* off great ideas from one industry and *Duplicating* them with her audiences.

Entertaining, Motivational "Speecher" Who Shares What Sizzles and Fizzles

Coming from humble beginnings and then almost going bankrupt in 2007, Liz poignantly shares how she rebuilt her business like the phoenix rising from the ashes. Dispelling business myths, she shares what really works in today's ADD, "always connected" world.

BONUS MATERIAL!

Register Your Book Today and Get Valuable Goodies and Bonus Material!

Since I practice what I speech, I don't want to just speak *at* you, but interact *with* you. Please register your book at www.speakgooder.com/bonus and use the code BONU$ to get bonus content and special goodies so that you can continue to speak gooder.

Register now and get:
- Samples of before-and-after bios to more easily write your bio.
- Sample of a fill-in-the-blank order handout that you can emulate.
- Example of my raffle forms so that you can create one too.
- Directions for setting up the room; create an option that works for you!
- Plus, sizzling insider secrets each week to move you forward.

I look forward to staying connected.
Liz Goodgold

CPSIA information can be obtained
at www.ICGtesting.com
Printed in the USA
FSOW04n1208261215
14624FS